Shame on You
You Were in My Dream

Ruth Velikovsky Sharon, Ph.D.

Copyright © 2003 by Ruth Velikovsky Sharon, Ph.D.

Internet: www.ruthvelikovskysharon.com
e-mail: ruthvsharonphd@verizon.net

All rights reserved. No part of this book may be reproduced or transmitted in any form or by any means, electronic or mechanical, including photocopying, recording, or by any information storage and retrieval system, without permission in writing from the copyright owner, except by reviewers who may quote brief passages to be printed in a magazine or newspaper.

Cover illustration: Ralph Schlegel

Published by   Paradigma Ltd.
                       Internet: www.paradigma-publishing.com
                       e-mail: info@paradigma-publishing.com

ISBN 978-1-906833-01-5

Contents

Preface 7
Publisher's Foreword 9
Introduction 13

I   X-Rated Movie 17
II   Dream Feelings 21
III Watch Out! 29
IV The Wrong Side of the Bed 35
V   I'm Manipulative 39
VI Empowering 49
VII Pleasant Dreams! 51
VIII Speak Up! 57
IX Catch My Dream! 61
X   Doctor Dreams 65
XI Dreams in Psychoanalytic Treatment 71
XII Essence 75
XIII Once Upon a Dream 79
XIV Pharaoh's Man 83
XV Dream Scape 89

Summary 95
Appendix: A New Understanding of Dreams 97
Index 105
Around the Subject 109

*To my children, Naomi, Rafael, Carmel
and my grandchildren
Elizabeth, Ashley, Cimarron,
Colby, Dylan, Canaan*

Preface

Dr. Ruth Velikovsky Sharon is the daughter of Dr. Immanuel Velikovsky, who is best known for his book *Worlds in Collision* – which in 1950 was outsold only by the bible.

A psychiatrist, her father, a collegue of Freud, Jung and Einstein published a paper reinterpreting Freud's dreams.

Influenced by her father, his daughter, a psychoanalyst, has developed a new approach to understanding dreams, which is both unique and brilliant, described in the chapters of this book.

Hyman Spotnitz, M.D.

Publisher's Foreword

Dreams – a familiar and enigmatic part or our life – accompany us night by night, whether we recall them consciously the next morning or not. At the same time they give rise to quite some thoughts, considerations, interpretations and at least just as many unconscious influences on our feelings and behavior. Sometimes promising, more often menacing, dreams have given the material for many a myth or legend in all cultures and periods.

Today, in the time of scientific investigation and analysis of the human psyche, their ambivalence has become even more apparent, and many theories have been made trying to give an explanation for the phenomenon of dreaming, also to be used as a basis for practical therapeutical application.

However, just as in other fields of science, the great number of existing theories, sometimes even contradicting each other, rather indicates that we are still at a loss for a well-founded, convincing and therefore generally accepted understanding.

The solution to such an unsatisfactory situation has often been a simple and straightforward recurrence to the basic laws of nature. This is what Dr. Sharon's new refreshing approach achieves. It does away with any complicated and speculative theoretical framework and just takes the dreams for what they basically are – a communication with (or from) our inner self about a problem for the dreamer. This simple approach is not only elegant, it opens up a fascinating way to many hitherto inexplicable cases and a whole new avenue to theoretical understanding and practical application alike.

That's why this book can give rise to one of the rare special feelings of awe, when you – unexpectedly – see a big and long-standing puzzle getting solved by a simple shift of the elements.

Paradigma Ltd.

*Thoughts are accompanied by visual images.
That awareness often comes as a surprise!
On that same "screen" dream images appear at night.
In daytime, the conscious has a say in what appears
on one's screen. At night, the unconscious takes over
in dreams.*

Introduction

Consider this thought: *Today is influenced by the dream I had last night, and the dream I have tonight will be influenced by what goes on today.* In other words, my day is colored by what I dreamt last night and what happens in my dream is about the struggles and problems I experience in my day. Every person, place and thing which appears in my dream – no matter how wonderfully the dream story may present them – in some way represents a problem or a struggle which I am experiencing in my immediate life. Nothing is exempt. No one is excused. You appear in my dream for a reason; the reason is that I have a problem with you! Tonight, my problems will appear in my dreams; tomorrow, my dreams will influence how I handle these problems.

Dreams are our closest companions. Though we may not consciously remember them, we retain our dreams in our unconscious, no matter where we are. If dream images are not there, dream feelings linger on like the Sirens song, compelling us to answer to those struggles and conflicts which we have avoided or ignored. Twenty-four hours a day, seven days a week, our dreams influence our thoughts and actions. How do dreams do this? And why?

Everything seen and heard in dreams reflects the dreamer's unresolved conflict or struggle in wakefulness. Dreams are about what is going on in the dreamer's physical and emotional life right now. Until the problem or conflict is solved, the dreamer will continue to dream about it and upon awakening, will carry that problem with him, perhaps acting on it in response to what he dreamed. At night, he will dream of the unresolved issue, which he brought with him to bed.

Just how long will this cycle continue? It will go on for as long as it takes for the problem in the dreamer's life to be solved. Sometimes problems are easy to solve; other times struggles are more persistent. They seem to dig into the fertile soil of the unconscious where they plant themselves and grow roots as pernicious as bamboo. In these cases, the dreamer struggles day and night with the same conflict manifesting itself over and over again.

As parents, we can help our children by listening to their dreams in order to understand and appreciate what it is that they are troubled by, and who troubles them. Their dream feelings and thoughts are telling us what it is that bothers them, what concerns them, what angers them, what frightens them. If you listen without judgment to what your child tells you went on in his head while he was asleep, you will learn what struggles your child is experiencing, which may open up a new understanding of what could be done to resolve your child's apprehensions, anxiety or worry. Learn to listen, listen to learn. When we ask a child: "What were you dreaming?" and "What were you thinking or feeling in your dream?" we are asking him to help us, as parents to recognize the problems that he wrestles with in wakefulness.

This should be good news to parents who may feel confused by a child's sudden change of behavior or mood. The child's dream holds important clues to the fears, the struggles and the problems which he is facing at this moment in his life.

In this book you will read about many different topics including how children use dreams to manipulate their parents, how dream feelings linger throughout the day and how our children's environment affects their dreams. Other subjects will include dreams as predictors of illness, dream experiences in children's books, why dream catchers don't work and why rewriting the end of one's dreams doesn't work. Though very different in content, each of these chapters offers a new way for parents to understand their children's dreams, as well as their own dreams.

Without resorting to an elaborate interpretive system, dreams can guide parents to important insights into their child's unconscious, for dreams reflect or duplicate the feeling of the predominant struggle of the child's immediate life, and the characters, situations and settings in the dream are inherently troubling to the child.

I
X-Rated Movie

Parents would not permit their young children to attend R or X-rated movies, yet, in the middle of the night, their children all by themselves in the privacy of their own "theaters", watch dreams often scarier than the scariest movie or television show.

Parents know very well that their children need no help from Hollywood to create for themselves in the dark of night, dreams that are more terrifying than anything that charges admission. Jenny and Jason can write, direct, produce, act in, and serve as casting agents for "movies" that are scary enough, thank you, without graphic input from the entertainment industry. Jenny and Jason can frighten themselves just fine with the special effects they create on their own. Children's imaginations need no stimulation from people whose profession is to think up new ways to horrify people. And of course, after concocting these movies, they wake their parents up in the middle of the night to complain that they are scared.

Unlike the general movie theaters, the child's unconscious does not censor dreams the way parents might wish it to. The unconscious allows the child to create and at once view these images which belong squarely to the dreamer's unconscious as a way of processing those problems and struggles which he is dealing with in everyday life.

In the dream the unconscious plays many roles. As writer, the unconscious prepares a script which enables the dreamer to express his concerns without everyday restrictions. As director, the unconscious decides what images will appear in each frame of the dream. In this role, too, the unconscious determines the overall feeling of the dream. The unconscious further acts as audience in the productions that take place several times each night. The dreamer not only produces and directs this movie, but casts every role, selects the filming locations, supervises the lighting and creates the special effects. The dreamer's unconscious chooses the props, designs the scenery, writes the screenplay and authors the script. The dreamer even determines whether the movie is in black and white or technicolor.

Figures in the dream are involuntary unpaid actors, cast because the dreamer has innate anger toward them. Scenery, animals and objects in the dream are all troubling to the dreamer in wakefulness. By casting a recognizable person, the dreamer reveals having a problem, such as anger, toward that person in wakefulness, even if the dream scenario does not indicate it. It is not an honor to be cast in another's dream. As casting agent, the unconscious chooses those people, places, and things which it believes are best suited to act out the dreamer's daytime problems.

Just as a writer decides what words will go into a script, and a director makes choices about lighting, framing, angles, mood, and many other aspects of movie-making, in dreams it is the job of the unconscious.

In all this the dreamer acts as the camera's eye. Everything is seen from his point of view, because *everything that appears in the dream represents a problem for the dreamer in wakefulness.* This bears repeating: There is nothing in a dream which does not signify a problem or struggle to the dreamer. When the dreamer appears visually in the dream – in front of the camera – the dreamer reveals a poor self-image in waking hours.

Why does the unconscious go to all this effort to produce a dream when there are no awards to be had, no financial gains to be made? The motivation behind the unconscious "movie" is to prod the dreamer toward new attitudes and to express feelings to others to whom the dream is reported without fearing retaliation.

Like movies, dreams have a larger-than-life quality. In dreams, we can escape gravity and time. We are now young, now old, with friends and strangers, where no sense makes sense and images are fragmented. But always behind are these questions: What is the predominant feeling? What is the thought during the dream? How does this connect with life? Seemingly random images taken from dreams are really perceptive documentaries of the dreamer's life. Sometimes dreams seem weird and difficult to understand. But they are full of important clues to the dreamer's life.

Will the unconscious create a dark, gloomy, haunting dream which manifests the dreamer's deep concerns? Or will it be a thrilling roller coaster adventure through strange lands reflecting anxiety? Whatever is included in the dream is troublesome to the dreamer. In dreams people are able to fly or levitate above situations that they prefer to avoid, they are intimate with people they probably shouldn't be intimate with. They speak with people who have died and come alarmingly close to dying themselves, or lose loved ones. They are tortured, chased, haunted, or tormented. They return to their childhood, to their old school, to a forgotten friend. Dreams are like shattered glass.

When parents create an environment that is open enough to encourage their children to share their dreams, they give their children – and themselves – a gift. That gift is the possibility of hearing their children's innermost thoughts, feelings, wishes and fears. And when those secrets are brought out into the light, then with the help of their parents, the children may be able to cope and even conquer problems that have been hidden in the unconscious. They will not need to be frightened of the "movies" that play in their heads while they sleep. Instead, they will see those dreams as educational, empowering and even sometimes entertaining tools

In addition, dreams shape our waking hours. Just like the aftermath of viewing a movie, dreams often leave the dreamer with a residue of feeling which he carries with him throughout the day, regardless of whether the dream is remembered. These feelings, lingering long into the day, can empower or cripple the dreamer.

II
Dream Feelings

Dreams linger like sunsets. There is an afterglow. This is true regardless of whether the dream is recalled. Random events may prompt the dreamer to remember what happened in his dream. Awakening in a good mood is the unconscious mind's constructive alarm clock which wakes up the dreamer at the moment of resolution in the dream so he can benefit from the good effect of the dream. The opposite side of this would be waking up irritable or agitated because of a dream.

Dreams are like mysteries, and dreamers upon waking up, look for clues. The feeling and thought in the dream duplicate the daytime struggle. Because the dream feeling remains present in the dreamer's mind, he may be able to figure out what the daytime struggle is, and begin to try to resolve it. The unconscious pictures the predicament or struggle in the dream in the same way the struggle is experienced in the dreamer's wakeful life. It's just that in the dream the people and places are different because the dream doesn't stick to what is real; it explores a *feeling* and *thought* that the dreamer struggles with.

If the dream includes feelings that are too intense for the dreamer to cope with during his waking hours, he might in daytime be motivated to race into some impulsive action. If, however, the dreamer wakes up disoriented and unable to think of any solutions to his struggle, he may avoid making an irreversible mistake. Sometimes the dreamer feels like he will explode from the intensity of feeling and the lack of a solution, so he withdraws into himself, "forgetting" both the dream and the problems it represents. However, the feeling will continue to hover over the day.

Chapter II

Life meets your child from both sides, coming and going. Your child responds to life. How he responds is mirrored in his dreams. If he can tell his dreams, and parents can listen, then there is a chance that both parties can move toward a constructive resolution of the child's concerns.

If the dreamer were to ask himself, "Where have I been?" after a night's dreams, the appropriate response would be: "With people I have issues with and in places I find problematic." The dream can open the door to issues and problems which plague the dreamer and, conversely, if the dreamer is not willing to journey into the dream, those issues and problems will play themselves out repeatedly and sleep will be no friend.

The unconscious mind puts together a dream to describe a thought or a feeling, which the dreamer is deeply effected by, and frequently is unable to identify. In this Never-Never Land, the unconscious creates a dream-riddle which enables the dreamer to get relief by "speaking" his feelings but also allows him to remain safe by disguising those feelings in the disjointed, fragmented language of dreams.

Parents could identify their child's main daytime struggle by pinpointing the feeling and thought in the child's dream, even if the story of the dream seems to have nothing to do with the child's struggle. If the child does not volunteer the feeling and thought he had in the dream the parent can ask: "What was your feeling in the dream?" It is rare that the child will not have an answer. For example: A five-year old can already identify being "scared". How a child feels, thinks and speaks in a dream helps the parent understand the child's unconscious mind. The dream reveals the emotion that is most important to the child at the time, which is made bigger by dream feelings, which don't just stop once the child wakes up. They linger throughout the day or longer regardless of whether the dream is recalled.

Dictionaries of dream symbols assembled in books and used by dreamers are subjective and presumptuous. The dream doesn't hold fast to the literal world; it explores the dreamer's emotional

Dream Feelings

being. It duplicates the feeling, thought and language of the major struggle in the dreamer's wakeful life.

Adults can distinguish, at least intellectually, between dreams and reality. They can dismiss movies and television shows as fabrications. Yet, the most assured, self-confident executive can awaken at night with his heart pounding, his palms sweating, his emotions seething, his dream so deeply troubling that he lies awake for an hour trying to recover from its emotional jolt. After all, even at the PG-13 level, the sex, violence and obscenity should be more than enough to disturb, or at least dismay, normal adults.

Sometimes dreams are so frightening that a child is awakened from sleep and seeks comfort; he either finds his way to his parents' room or calls for the parent to come to him. Either way, everyone's sleep is interrupted. How many adults remember that as children, they were shown that there was no monster under the bed? Nobody in the closet? How many adults remember being told that everything was fine, go back to bed? But how many adults also remember being unable to explain why everything wasn't fine? Why simply being reassured of the absurdity of the dream did not help very much?

If a child is permitted to crawl into the parent's bed or the parent sleeps in the child's room because the child has had a nightmare, nightmares are encouraged. If the child appears in the doorway of the parents' bedroom in the middle of the night, the parent should lead the child back to his room and then promptly return to his own bed. Although nightmares are frightening, parents should not suppress them by telling their children not to dream, nor invite the children into their bed in order to "prevent" nightmares.

As already stated the dream story will not necessarily include the identical people, places, and things present in the conscious struggle, because dreams don't stick to what is real; they explore the feelings and thoughts that the dreamer is dealing with. However, they will present the same problems and struggles which the dreamer experiences because everything in dreams represents a problem or an issue to the dreamer in wakefulness. The dreamer's predominant feeling and thought, and the language in the dream mirror the dreamer's life circumstance.

While the dream preserves much of the dreamer's reality, the unconscious often changes names and faces. The struggle in the dream is the struggle the dreamer is experiencing in wakeful life, although some of the people and places may be unfamiliar. A double phenomena takes place. The feeling, thought and scenario depict the dreamer's struggle, while the characters and locations represent a problem to the dreamer. These two phenomena work hand in hand. The dream doesn't hold fast to the literal world; it explores the dreamer's feelings and concerns of the major struggle in the dreamer's wakeful life.

Dream theorists suggest that children benefit from embracing the nightmare, becoming a part of it, or rewriting the events and the conclusion. However, since nightmares are an expression of the dreamer's unconscious, re-writing the ending of a dream once awake, interferes with the creative work of the unconscious. Pretending that the nightmare had a happy ending is self-deception and a useless exercise. There is a reason why a person dreams of a particular series of events with a disturbing "ending". Helping the child resolve his daytime struggle will genuinely create a "happy ending". It will be the work of the creator of the nightmare – the unconscious.

Dream Feelings

Dream Examples duplicating the daytime struggle and predominant feeling:

☁ A young boy who felt unappreciated and mistreated even though he tried to make friends on the school playground, dreamt that he helped a physically and emotionally handicapped boy disembark from the school bus. No one on the bus appreciated his good deed, and as the handicapped boy successfully got off the bus, he squeezed the dreamer's hand, causing him pain.

☁ A girl dreamt she was looking at a photograph and was undecided whether it was a picture of her deceptive friend or of a stranger. Her feeling of uncertainty about her friend's identity and deceptive nature was re-created in the dream.

☁ A young girl who tried to get a stubborn friend to listen to her suggestions about how to get a passing grade, dreamt she instructed her friend to go around to the other side of the car and get in, but to no avail. The feeling in the dream was disappointment at her friend's stubbornness.

☁ A boy who thought his father was not trustworthy dreamt that he was sitting in his father's illegally parked car, while observing his father driving another car the wrong way and making an illegal U-turn. The feeling in the dream was one of mistrust.

☁ A girl whose relationship to her mother was very antagonistic, and who thought her mother went "too far" with her rebuking, dreamt a taxi driver took her past her destination. In her dream, she thought, "The driver went too far." In a second dream a menacing black dog lunged at her and blocked the gate to her yard. The feeling in the dream was danger from a source that was out of control. As her relationship with her mother continued to deteriorate, the girl dreamt that the leather on the heel of her shoe was beyond repair. The thought in the dream was that the "heel" could not be salvaged.

💭 A boy dreamt that his cat faded into a skeleton and that he did nothing to prevent it. He identified the feeling of guilt in the dream which, in waking hours he experienced about neglecting his little brother.

💭 A girl, astonished by the news that her father and mother were about to be divorced, dreamt that her deceased grandfather, out of character, had straggly hair and was seated at a bar. The girl described the feeling of astonishment at her grandfather's appearance and behavior.

💭 A patient dreamt she lost her valuable gold necklace and kept hoping she would find it, but realized that it was almost hopeless. In actuality the necklace had been misplaced then located and was safe at home. In life she was despondent about her husband's treatment of her. Her husband had given her the necklace years before.

The dream crystallized the difficult feelings she was dealing with. She used the recent misplacement of the necklace to communicate her predominant feeling in life, one of uncertainty and hopelessness. She was a recent breast cancer victim, having lost a breast, she remained uncertain about her health and prognosis. The hopelessness reported in the dream described her predominant feeling in life.

💭 A man reported dreaming that he was running alone in Central Park. The feeling in the dream was fear of being mugged. In life the man was afraid of being financially mugged by his wife who was about to separate from him.

Dream Feelings

☁ A woman felt relieved to have saved her job at the last possible moment before being fired. She dreamt she retrieved her dentures just in the nick of time as a maid reached to pick them up. The feeling in the dream was relief at having prevented a loss.

☁ A divorced man had unprotected sex, and fearing AIDS, thought his life was in danger. He dreamt that he jumped out of a second story window into a swimming pool trying to save his son from drowning. The thought in the dream "I could have killed myself," duplicated the thought in wakefulness.

☁ A woman who felt that her son had made a foolhardy, irreversible decision at his job, dreamt she was living in an unsuitable apartment which her husband had leased. The thought in the dream was that a foolhardy, irreversible decision had been made.

☁ A movie director who was apprehensive about the success of his upcoming movie, dreamt that his sister was shot. He described the feeling of apprehension about whether she would live or die.

III
Watch Out!

If someone says, "I had a dream about you last night!" – watch out! It is not an honor to be cast in another person's dream. Why? Because when the dreamer casts someone familiar in a dream it means that he has a problem or an issue with that person when awake, even though the dream story may not show it. "Actors" in a dream do not choose to be there; they have been cast because the dreamer has a problem with them. Whereas it could be as simple as an issue of not seeing them often enough – the problems cover a range of feelings from animosity and anger to unrequited affection. Regardless, these actors are responsible for appearing in another's dream: They are doing something in life to upset the dreamer.

Every character in a dream presents a problem to the dreamer during waking hours. By casting a recognizable person, the dreamer reveals having a problem or anger toward that person in wakefulness, *even if the person is portrayed positively in the dream.*

This is a hard concept for many people to accept, for dreams have long been interpreted as expressions of wishes and desires. Evidence of this abounds in everyday conversation: "He is the man of my dreams." "It's a dream house." "This car steers like a dream." "I can dream, can't I?" Though the word "dream" is commonly used to convey the idea of desirable or wonderful, according to this theory such associations are not accurate. A character in a dream who is helpful, and a friend, nevertheless is there because the dreamer has a problem or an issue with that person. If Jason dreams that Dad is helping him with his homework, the homework is difficult for Jason and needing help from his Dad is a problem. Dream emotion reflects the dreamer's feeling concerning a real problem or dilemma in his life rather than a wish fulfillment.

When the recognizable figure in the dream is deceased, the dreamer's unresolved feelings have followed that person to the grave. Unidentifiable people in the dream signal the dreamer has a problem with strangers. All images in the dream, including locations, races and religions are problems for the dreamer in wakefulness. This includes representations of the dreamer himself. Although the dreamer most often is the camera's eye in each dream, when appearing in full view, the dreamer has issues with himself in daytime.

Every image which appears in the dream is a problem or an issue to the dreamer. It's a screen where the dreamer deals with his frustrations, dislikes, disappointments, enemies and complaints. It's like a black book where the dreamer keeps a running list of all the people that are problematic to him in daytime. He then casts them in his dreams. They don't audition. They are simply assigned a role whether they want to appear in another's dream or not. They are not there by choice and by appearing in someone's dream, they are "guilty" in the dreamer's mind of having done something wrong in daytime.

If the dream depicts scenes of being loving or being loved in the dream, it may point to what the dreamer feels he *lacks* in his wakeful life – which is a problem or an issue to the dreamer.

Where do the seemingly unrelated images, which float around in dreams, come from? A dream is made up of images, memories, feelings and thoughts that have been stored in the dreamer's unconscious. The dreamer seems to sort through and find the appropriate pictures to express the feelings and problems with which the dreamer is struggling.

When a person dreams the same dream over and over, he not only has a problem with the people and places in the dream, he also thinks of himself as unimaginative, having created the same "movie" over and over again.

Sometimes we don't know what our problems are or how deeply they affect us. But our dreams do because they are being coached by our unconscious. The unconscious is like Puck, a spirit in Shakespeare's *A Midsummer Night's Dream*. Puck knows what everyone dreams. He knows what worries the dreamer. He knows how hard it is for the dreamer to express his troubles in daytime, who needs to hear those concerns and how to get the message across.

Parents might ask their children, "What did you dream?"; "What were you thinking or feeling in the dream?" It is best for parents to be available to hear and be accepting of the child's dream. It doesn't help to attempt to interpret to the child his dream nor to ask questions for clarification of what took place in what order. The child's recollection of what he dreamt – how he felt during the dream and what he thought – are important. In addition, the language the child uses to report the dream is significant. When a parent has an interpretation of his child's dream, he should withhold all comments, so the child's dreams will not be affected by the parent's reactions.

An experience that many parents share is being woken up in the night by a child who is having a bad dream. In the middle of the night, a child cries out terrified. When his parent goes to calm him, the child says that he was having a nightmare. He is very, very frightened. The parent puts the child back to bed then returns to his own troubled sleep.

What is this all about? The child's unconscious forms a dream around the need to let someone important know he is having a problem. Many times, especially with children, that particular person is the parent. Suppose you are the parent. What goes on for you? Your sleep is interrupted, something which could be seen as an unconsciously hostile act on the child's part. He is pushing his way into your own private time and taking away your own necessary sleep.

When parents appear in their children's dreams with an "assigned script" no less, and the script is disturbing to the child who made it up and dreamt it, the parents nevertheless are blamed.

Although the parents could get incensed, the children are justified, since whatever and whoever appears in their dream is a problem to the dreamer in daytime. That makes the parents accountable for their daytime relationship to their child, and they are automatically "incriminated" when they appear in their children's dreams.

Children often dream about their parents, sometimes in frightening ways. "You just dropped me off outside my new school and drove away!" says Jenny one morning. "You didn't go in with me. I got lost and couldn't find my classroom, so I went to the basement. It was all dark and dirty, and then people were scolding me. I was crying so hard!" Jenny's parents, hearing how their child has cast them in her dream, are disturbed by what she – her unconscious – has made up. They feel unjustly blamed and protest with logical arguments: "But Jenny, you know we'd never do that. We would always go in with you on the first day. And the people there are very nice and wouldn't scold you." And so on. However, it is her parents' responsibility to remember that whatever and whoever appeared in Jenny's dream is a problem to her in daytime. This includes her school, no doubt, and her parents themselves. Jenny has no way to control what her unconscious does with those problems when she is dreaming. However, her parents may be able to help her by listening carefully when she tells them her dreams.

But while they remind Jenny that her teacher likes her and would never make her stand outside in the snow, and as they comfort Jason that their house is built very solidly and can't fall down, do they remember that those same assurances they heard as children didn't help – not one bit? Do they remember how hard it was to get back into that bed, how logic and assurances and humor didn't seem to matter much as they lay surrounded by those vague nighttime shadows? Perhaps they do remember, but as adults, they are influenced by what is familiar and effective in their adult relationships, so they resort to the same assurances and explanations and reasoning that failed them when they were young. Well, they'll explain things better, more rationally and convincingly than their parents did with them. After all, what else can they do? Kids have always had bad dreams and always will. It's part of life. But they grow up. Yes, and they still have bad dreams.

When children tell their parents their dreams, they are presenting them with a chance to get to know them better, to understand them, to recognize their problems. Parents should note a wonderful opportunity when a tearful Jenny appears at their bedside, or Jason says, "I had a bad dream!" The unconscious allows the child to create and at once view these images which belong squarely to the dreamer's unconscious, as a way of processing those problems and struggles which deal with everyday life.

IV
The Wrong Side of the Bed

Regardless of a person's awareness of having dreamt, waking up "on the wrong side of the bed" hints at having had a disturbing dream. If the dreamer can go back to sleep, and have a "better" dream, the initial "damage" could get repaired and he may wake up in a better mood.

It is all pervasive and disturbing to be subjected to the bad mood of a person who awakens from a bad dream and takes his emotional baggage with him all day, dropping bits and pieces along the way. Nonverbal communication, such as body language or facial expressions can send out a message: "Beware! I had a bad dream."

Dreams shape our waking hours empowering or crippling. Dream feelings linger throughout the day or longer, regardless of whether the dream is recalled. Daytime decisions are made and roadblocks to creativity are either removed or erected as a result of a feeling or thought in a dream having ignited urgency.

The plot of the dream depicts a particular situation, which *represents* the dreamer's most significant experience in waking hours. The people appearing in the dream have a double function: The first is to serve as actors and the second is to alert the dreamer that they represent problems to the dreamer in daytime, since *everything that appears in a dream represents a problem to the dreamer!* While all this is going on, what does the dreamer do? Often the dreamer acts as the camera's eye, an onlooker, where everything is seen from the dreamer's point of view, while the dreamer is being helped by the unconscious to recognize the main problem and struggle in his life.

The dream story will not necessarily include the people, places, and things which represent the daytime struggle, because dreams don't stick to what is real; the child's recollected dream is like a game of charades where the dreamer is asked to identify the predominant feeling and thought in the dream, which invariably is the predominant feeling and thought the dreamer struggles with. The unconscious hides its secrets from the conscious and only releases clues to puzzles and riddles, which the conscious mind is ill equipped to solve. Nevertheless, the conscious tries to maintain sanity by releasing symbols and images during dreams. Upon awakening the unconscious stores the dream images along with a myriad other images.

There is an aspect which reads like Zen Koan. Today is influenced by the dream I had last night, and the dream I had last night is I influenced by today. In other words, what goes on in my dream is about what went on in my day, and what went on in my day was about what went on in my dream.

What happens when children don't get enough sleep?

Night terrors are often confused with nightmares, but the two are very different. Night terrors are a biological phenomenon, and so they do not fall into the category of manipulative tools; however, parents who are not familiar with this state may find it useful to know what night terrors look like and how to handle them.

Many young children experience night terrors. These differ from nightmares because the child actually seems awake, but it is just the opposite. Night terrors occur during stage 3/4 in the sleep cycle, when the child is in the deepest sleep. Parents are usually alerted to a child's night terror when the child screams out loud in a shrill or agitated voice. One parent describes her daughter's night terrors this way: "She seemed really scared and confused, and she said things I couldn't understand. When I tried to reach out to her, she jerked back from me as if she was terrified of me, her eyes were open so wide, and she crashed into the wall behind her bed. I was so scared for her, and for me, it made me want to cry."

Teens who have sleep problems generally exhibit daytime physical, behavioral and emotional problems. These can include anything from sleepiness, fatigue, headaches and weakness to anxiety, tantrums, attention deficit disorder and depression. They might even show signs of antisocial behavior.

Hormonal and physical changes during puberty could make preteens extra sleepy, as sleep becomes increasingly important. Also during puberty a child's sleep cycles change. It is during delta sleep, the period of deep sleep, which occurs during the first third of the night, that the human growth hormone is released. If sleep is severely impaired, as in cases of sleep apnea and insomnia, the normal secretion of the hormone is disrupted. Doctors believe that this may impede growth.

The cost of not sleeping well is monumental. Seventy million Americans suffer from sleep disorders. The cost of treating sleep disorders has boosted the national health bill by $15.9 billion.

Every year hundreds of accidents occur as a result of sleep deprivation. One in six fatal road accidents are attributed to fatigue. The cost of these accidents cannot just be figured in dollars and cents. The lives of people, wildlife and great chunks of nature were destroyed. The 1989 Exxon Valdez oil spill in Alaska is thought to have resulted from human error and fatigue. The Challenger space shuttle disaster and the Chernobyl nuclear accident have both been attributed to human error and linked to sleep deprivation. These are all accidents that might not have happened if the humans involved had enjoyed sleep uninterrupted.

Consider the cost of not getting enough sleep. According to CNN, 70,000,000 Americans suffer from these consequences of sleep deprivation: tiredness, lack of focus, irritability, frustration, and impulsive emotional behavior.

Not sleeping, means not dreaming and therefore having no outlet for pent up emotions.

V
I'm Manipulative!

We often think of a manipulative person as one who acts out of maliciousness or greed. However, manipulation in a person's dream is a tool. It is a shield that the dreamer uses to fend off what he perceives as a potential threat. It's neither maliciousness nor greed. How is a dream manipulative? *It is manipulative because the dreamer is not coming right out and saying what he is feeling.* He is using a dream as a tool of communicating.

However, children who have a hard time saying what they are thinking and feeling – perhaps because they are suffering from the pains of maturing, perhaps because they have been discouraged by their parents or others from speaking freely – may feel safe to express an "unsafe" thought or feeling from a dream. Communicating what took place in a dream, rather than pointing a finger of accusation at the parents, the dream protects the child from possible, in some cases, probable confrontation with an authority figure. The dream, in a sense, can be used as an opportunity to communicate fears and anger in safety.

Besides sharing the dialogue and story of their dreams as children do, adults have all sorts of manipulative ways of communicating what they find difficult to say. They "say it with flowers," sending huge bouquets in place of words that they cannot express. Or they rely on Hallmark cards on a special anniversary or holiday. If they have difficulty with intimacy, they may resort to cooking gourmet meals or give a gift of jewelry. After all, aren't diamonds a girl's best friend and isn't the stomach the quickest way to a man's heart?

What if the feeling is one of embarrassment, anger, guilt, or fear? These are more difficult feelings to express because there is always that "What if?" in the background. "What if I lose control?"; "What if they lose control?" Whatever the answer to these questions, most children don't have control over these "ifs". So how do children and adults make their really important feelings known? Through their dreams. A child can use a dream to express anger without being afraid of the people to whom the dream is reported, since reporting a dream shields the child from responsibility or culpability. To sum it up, reporting the dream can be manipulative.

If adults are resourceful, children are even more so, which isn't such a bad thing, because it is how many children have managed to survive.

The unconscious may form a dream based on the child's need to express a powerful feeling to a significant person in the child's life. The dream story motivates the child to tell the content to the person who appeared in the dream.

It is not by mistake that the phrase "I am at a loss for words" is firmly embedded in our culture. Sometimes we simply do not know what to say in response to a pleasant situation like a party thrown by our closest friends, or a disturbing one marking a profoundly unsettling situation which renders one speechless. The bombing of the World Trade Center Towers and the Pentagon on September 11, 2001, left most of the country without the words to say what we felt and continued to feel for days, weeks, and months after.

Our children – what they say and do – often leave us speechless. We think of them as being refreshing, open, and saying whatever it is that pops up in their minds.

As an example a four-year-old boy and his father were walking in a park. This was in the days before tattoos, body piercing, metal studded leather, and fluorescent hair were commonplace. But walking toward the crowd was just such a figure, tall and lanky, dressed in a black leather vest and pants with gleaming metal studs, and sporting a tall, spiked comb of crimson hair. As this creature strode across the yard, the crowd drew back, except

I'm Manipulative

the little boy who stopped and gazed up at the brilliant crimson comb on the fellow's head. Then the little boy turned to his father and said, "Look, Daddy, it's a big chicken!" Who but a child would have said such a thing? Not because he was exceptionally clever or brave, but because he was confident that he could. He probably never gave it a second thought.

There are times when children, especially as they get older, feel the constraints and censoring and they cannot put their feelings into words, when they have feelings and problems that plague them. Sometimes they are not consciously aware of their problems which they cannot express. So how do they express their feelings? Sometimes they use their dreams.

The parents who "jump the gun" and share with the child their thoughts about the child's dreams, may prevent the child from freely associating his own thoughts to his dream. It is best for the parent to simply ask, "What was your feeling or thought in the dream?" and after receiving the answer, "Thanks for telling me your dream." Nothing more!

People who are unaware, unable or unwilling to say what they are thinking may report a thought, feeling or language from a dream for the purpose of releasing hostility without fearing the wrath of those to whom the dream is reported. Dreams shield from responsibility and therefore create an opportunity for manipulation. In repeating the story of a dream, the child takes license to express feelings circumventing inhibition.

An eleven-year-old boy was unable to express his feeling of anxiety about the attacks on the World Trade Center Towers. Instead, he relayed the following dream several days after the event:

 First I was in a volcano being blown up, and then I was in a guillotine about to have my head cut off, and then I was in a tunnel being chased by a monster, and then I was in a tall building that was falling apart. But it wasn't one of the World Trade Center Towers.

This dreamer recalled being scared in his dream and thinking that he was going to die. Reporting the dream feeling to his parents relieved his anxiety.

An anxiety-ridden young girl who was suffering from a congenital disease told her mother her dream where she was in a store and a song titled "Please Don't Give Up On Me" played over a loud speaker. The young girl didn't feel the freedom to express these words to her mother without the words supplied by her dream. She then proceeded to tell the dream to several other people, all of whom she felt needed to hear her plea: "Please don't give up on me."

The child's unconscious uses diverse means to manipulate his parents while the child sleeps and dreams. Dreams bring to the forefront the child's unexpressed feelings. When a child wakes and tells his parent his dream, he unknowingly (unconsciously) frequently assaults the parents. If the parents think that the child sounds hostile or accusatory, the child then can claim his innocence. After all, he was only dreaming! If in the dream, one character says certain words to another character, and the dreamer repeats these words the listeners' unconscious could hear the words as directed at them.

Dreams, especially dreams like these, are highly manipulative. In these dreams, the unconscious forms a story around the need to express a powerful feeling or problem to someone, and the dream motivates the dreamer to tell the dream to that person. If, in wakefulness, the child perceives the parent as unreceptive to whatever the child might express, and he anticipates a negative response to his negative feelings, the child, to avoid his parents' rebuke, hides his anger, leaving it well hidden in the trenches of his unconscious. After all, what child can embrace a parent's rejection? The dream comes to the rescue, providing the child with a safe outlet for his feelings. The dream essentially is an enabler. It enables the child to indirectly confront the parents with "forbidden" words.

Consider the characters of "Iago" in Shakespeare's *Othello* or, on a less elevated level, "Alexis Carrington" in the television show

I'm Manipulative

Dynasty. These are people who manipulated events to get what they felt they were entitled to. Manipulation in a child's dream, however, is a tool. It is a shield that the child uses to fend off what he perceives as a potential threat.

In Greek mythology, the young man Perseus had to accomplish the almost impossible task of beheading the Gorgon Medusa. (He did this in order to honor his mother's wish not to marry King Polydectes.) The Gorgon was a formidable adversary, for anyone who even glanced at Medusa turned to stone. However, Perseus knew to ask for help, which he received from the goddess Athene. With her help, he obtained a pair of winged sandals (to fly), a cap of darkness (to become invisible), and a sword. What did he bring of his own? A bronze shield. Despite all the other tools, it was the shield which enabled him to look at the monster indirectly without being turned to stone and to lop off her head, thus fulfilling his goal.

A child's dream experience is not unlike Perseus' journey. The child flies on the wings of sleep in the black of night into worlds where he confronts a variety of emotions - anger, disillusionment, attraction, fear and countless others. Often in his dreams he is invisible, only watching as the dream story unfolds. The dreamer may be afraid not only of the "monsters" which he is confronting, but also of the reaction of the people to whom he wants to report the dream This dream shield allows the child to do so.

There are times, however, when children cannot put their feelings into words, when they have feelings and problems that plague them which they cannot express. Or, they may simply be unaware of what they are feeling and use dreams to protect themselves from expressing feelings that might be seen as unacceptable.

A ten-year-old boy who felt threatened by his father's anger had this dream:

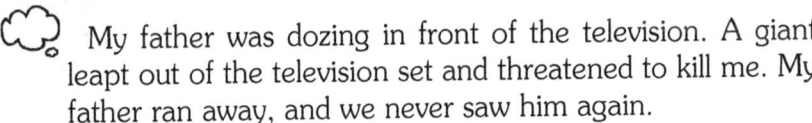 My father was dozing in front of the television. A giant leapt out of the television set and threatened to kill me. My father ran away, and we never saw him again.

This boy used his dream to express his anger. If his father were to raise his hand against the boy upon hearing the dream, the boy could say, "But Dad, it was just a dream!" In this way, the boy is using the dream as a manipulative tool.

Somebody once said, "Sure our children know how to push our buttons, they should, they installed them." In dreams the unconscious gives the child total freedom to explore the feelings that he can't express in his waking life. Then, it gives the child words and the way to tell the dream to the person who "needs" to hear it. How is this manipulative? If the words are hurtful or blaming, the child doesn't have to take any responsibility for the dream.

Words that are part of a dream scenario, whether spoken by the dreamer or character in the dream, are communications the child is unwilling to verbalize directly to the parent. The same process occurs when a child cries out or speaks out in his sleep as a result of a disturbing dream. He is afraid that speaking negative thoughts and feelings will get him in trouble with the person who is listening. He may also be afraid of what will happen to him if he lets the words flow out of his mouth. When the child suffers from night terror, it is more of an aggressive act, since the child does not use words. The child who reports his dream is less afraid of his surroundings than the child who suffers from night terror.

When children don't know how to talk to their parents about an important feeling or concern, they sometimes resort to dreams. Now, this isn't a conscious choice. It is a natural result of the situation in which the dreamer finds himself. The child's unconscious can create a dream based on the child's need to express a powerful feeling to the parents. Because of the overriding feeling of the dream, the child cannot hold it inside; he feels that he must communicate the dream. There may be a character in the dream who says words which the child is unable to say directly to the parent. Where does the language in the dream come from and how does the child get the ability to talk while sleeping? A child stores myriad "pictures" and images in his brain which can be assigned into a dream by the child's unconscious. He is able to

I'm Manipulative

say what he could not say before because now he has an alibi. He can claim innocence saying, "It was only a dream." Even though the parents may hear the words directed at them, the child is "off the hook." The same process occurs when a child cries or speaks out as a result of a disturbing dream.

A young girl who had animosity for her mother because of a birthmark on her own face had a dream in which one person said to another, "I hate you. I'll never forgive you," words she could never say to her mother. When she had the dream to fall back on, she was able to repeat the dream and its language to her mother. This can be seen as manipulative, for her mother felt attacked by the words her daughter used when reporting her dream.

Dreams can open the door to issues and problems which plague the child. Conversely, if the child is afraid to journey into the dream and repeat the dream language, those issues and problems will play themselves repeatedly and sleep will be no friend.

Dreams often compel the child to share them. This creates an opportunity for unconscious communication and raises the following question: Does the unconscious mind create a dream for the purpose of surreptitiously communicating with people to whom the dream will be reported? Are dreams formed to communicate a particular message to people in the dreamer's life? Does a child's unconscious form a dream around a child's need to express a powerful feeling or problem to someone and the dream motivates the child to tell the dream to that person and other people as well, who the dreamer feels need to hear the message?

Is the unconscious so crafty as to purposely manufacture language in a dream, which, when removed from the dream scenario, will communicate what the person wants to say to another in wakefulness?

☁ A girl dreamt that despite her pleas to her friend in her dream, "Talk to me! Talk to me!" her friend refused to talk to her. In reporting the dream language, the girl indirectly pleaded with anyone to whom she told the dream. All she had to say was: I had a dream last night where I asked a friend to 'Talk to me!' which was ammunition to use with people she wanted should talk to her.

☁ A boy who suspected his parents had kept a secret from him throughout his life reported to his parents what he said in his dream to his friend: "I knew where you were, but I did not know where you were. I would have been hurt to know where you were. I did not care to know where you were." He used the dream language to give a warning to his parents that he did not want the information.

☁ A young girl, too shy to ask for what she wanted, dreamt she bought a designer dress she could not afford. She reported the dream to a family member who, she knew, upon hearing the dream, would buy her a designer dress, which, in fact, the family member did.

☁ A girl who complained that her parents basically ignored her, reported a dream of "taking cancer pills." The dream startled her alarmed parents into paying attention to her.

☁ A young girl reported several dreams where everyone was mean to her. Born with a congenital illness, the predominant feeling was that no matter how nice family members were to her, they were all mean for not "taking away" her illness. She regularly reported to her mother dreams where "everyone was mean to me." Having used the word "everyone" it included her mother, at whom she indirectly released anger for her illness.

I'm Manipulative

☁ A young boy, angry at his mother, dreamt that his deceased grandfather was alive. In his dream his mother exclaimed, "He's been alive but he never came to see us." In reporting the dream to his mother, the young boy attacked her by creating painful memories.

☁ A young boy told his father a dream in which he said to his father, "I am angry at you." In reporting the dream language to his father, he released anger, free of fearing his father retaliating.

☁ A vindictive young teenager dreamt that three of his friends from school were in a car. He took a gun and shot all of them. He then added, "It felt good to kill," unsettling and forewarning anyone to whom he told the dream, that he, in fact, was someone to fear.

☁ A young boy was upset that his dentist had filled three cavities in one visit but was afraid to speak up. The next night he said out loud in his sleep, "Don't aim it at me!" Although he could not recall specifics from the dream, he made the connection between the dream and his daytime struggle, and in telling his parents the dream he sought their help with his next dental visit.

☁ A wealthy yet frugal young woman who paid for several family members' therapy sessions, dreamt the analyst gave her a break with the fee for two family members. Reporting the dream to the analyst gave her a manipulative opportunity to bring the subject up with the analyst.

☁ A young woman did not know how to approach a relative for financial assistance. Since timing was crucial, she dreamt that she said to her relative, "I have to ask you for financial help because of a deadline." In the dream the relative hesitated. The young woman dealt with the momentary rejection in the dream content, and was thus prepared for any negative reaction from the relative. The dream was a dress rehearsal. She was then able to tell the relative the dream which provided her with the confidence and the language to ask for what she wanted.

VI
Empowering

People aren't the only targets zeroed in by the dreamer. Sometimes the dreamer will dream about an upcoming event in order to get a handle on the feelings and thoughts surrounding that event. How many times have we heard of the pre-exam dream in which the dreamer arrives late or at the wrong place or forgets everything and can't answer the questions? Having dreamt this, the dreamer will then in daytime make every attempt to arrive on time at the right place and know the answers. If a dream about an upcoming event includes people, by their being in his dream, they are problems to the dreamer and the dream may prepare and fortify the dreamer to deal with the people and the event.

Dreams affect behavior and feelings in daytime, either providing inertia to solving problems or "paralyzing" the dreamer into inaction when impulsive action would be counter indicated. A dream may provoke action and change attitudes in the face of particularly difficult issues in the dreamer's life. Such dreams can be seen as self-manipulation designed to provoke a response in the dreamer, prodding him toward new attitudes and actions.

> A young woman dreamt of people fighting. She awakened disoriented and in emotional "paralysis," unable to get out of bed for several hours, thereby keeping herself from initiating destructive action.

> A boy who was enraged with a friend who had mistreated him, expected to see the friend at a school assembly. The night before the event the boy had a pleasant dream about the former friend, leading to the temporary resolution of the negative feelings toward the former friend, enabling him to tolerate the event while behaving properly.

☁ A young girl did not know how to tell her parents about receiving poor grades in school. In her dream she said to her parents, "I have to ask you for help." In the dream the parents hesitated, causing the girl to have to deal with the momentary rejection. The dream was a "dress rehearsal", which provided her with the confidence and the language to ask for what she needed. Having experienced rejection in her dream, anticipating experiencing it again was not anxiety provoking.

☁ A young boy tried in vain to get his father to tell him to bring his sick cat into the house. The father refused. The boy then dreamt that his father told him to bring the cat in the house, which he proceeded to do the next day, free of pangs of conscience, insisting "I dreamt you told me to bring Fuzzy into the house!"

☁ An eight-year-old girl whose mother was periodically institutionalized for emotional illness dreamt that her grandmother sat in the backseat of a car while her mother was driving uphill. Suddenly, her mother was no longer driving and the car was driving itself. The girl's anger towards her grandmother, who the girl felt was responsible for her mother's emotional illness, was temporarily resolved by telling her grandmother the dream.

VII
Pleasant Dreams!

How successful are a parent's bedtime instructions to a child? Can one act like a fullback and thwart a dream? Telling a child to dream pleasant dreams, to dream about a certain topic, to recall his dreams, or not to dream at all will control the wealth of the unconscious. Releasing incoherent thoughts and words via dreams, helps sanity reign in wakefulness. Telling a child to write down his dreams in the morning will make him self-conscious while dreaming, consequently controlling the dreams. Dreams release "insane" energy and therefore should not be subjected to instruction and thereby, control.

At bedtime, although parents wish their children "sweet dreams," their children often disobey and persist in having bad dreams, awakening the parents and disturbing everyone's sleep. Parents often get upset when, after wishing their children "pleasant dreams", their children have nightmares and awaken the parents. All of this seeming defiance can frustrate parents, who have taken great care to ease their children into a land of warm fuzzy dreams. Especially frustrating is the child who wakes up from a nightmare in the middle of the night and no amount of checking under the bed and looking in the closet for monsters, or coaching him to think good thoughts seems to change the nature of the child's dreams. When parents tell their children not to dream at all, the children often defy them. These parents are missing a critical point: the child's unconscious uses the dream to express immediate problems and struggles as well as to release disconnected images. Any attempt to control the child's dreams shuts down this outlet and puts the child at emotional risk. It is best to simply say "good night" and make no reference to dreams. Any recommendations about dreaming is counter productive.

When parents interfere with their children's dream life – by being too instructive at night or too inquisitive in the morning – they introduce a new dimension of intrusion into their children's unconscious life. The result is a child who is self-conscious and self-aware while dreaming, thereby controlling his dreams or ending his dreams and as a result limiting the release of emotional tension while dreaming. Self-conscious awareness of dreaming, and observing oneself in "one's own movie" destroys the child's potential of using dreams as a therapeutic tool of communicating with their parents. It is best to simply say "good night" at bedtime and "good morning" when the child rises. It is not recommended to say: "Sweet dreams!"; "Dream about your new bike"; "Write down your dreams in the morning"; "Keep a dream journal" or "Draw a picture of your dream in the morning."

When a dream is interrupted by a pause of awareness it obstructs the free outpouring of tension in dreams. The conscious thought in the dream "I am dreaming", keeps the unconscious from creating a free-flowing dream and cuts off the wealth of images flowing from the unconscious. These images need to be filtered out during dreams but instead they clutter up the dreamer's mind.

☁ A girl dreamt that she told her little sister that their summer home was about to be sold. The girl was apprehensive about her little sister's reaction to the news. However, the little sister's calm reaction in the dream enabled the older sister to, free of trepidation, warn her little sister of the impending sale.

☁ A young girl dreamt that she went on a trip with her parents who forgot her clothes and refused to retrieve them. Feeling little control over her life, she woke herself out of the dream, thus ending the suffering in the dream and, with it, the farther outpouring of unconscious material. Her ability to awaken herself demonstrated her attempt to control her life.

💭 A boy who felt unsettled because his father was angry with him, dreamt that he was going up an Empire State Building elevator and the elevator tipped from side to side. He felt unsettled as his conscious overpowered his unconscious and he woke himself up, putting an end to the dream and, with it, the bad feelings.

Not realizing that their children's "bad" dreams release tensions and contain important messages which need to be expressed and explored, parents take extreme measures to try to induce in their children "sweet dreams". If parents use measures such as rocking, singing or lying down with the child to encourage sleep, bad habits are formed that will be difficult to break when the child is older. A stuffed animal or a blanket – are all "security blankets" for little children. However, does he wear special pajamas with a super hero on the front who will protect him from bad dreams? Does he sleep on sheets of clouds and stars? Or have you put a herd of day glo sheep over his bed so that he can count them as he falls asleep? A child who is afraid of going to sleep, having had scary dreams, only has his fears reinforced by these measures as well as by hanging dream catchers to fabricate placid dreams. All these measures send the message: "We want you to have only happy dreams (life)," rather than: "We want you to be strong enough to deal with whatever life doles out – the good, the bad and the difficult."

For a parent to give a child the message that dreams somehow can and should be censored is a destructive message. Dreams are the place where children's problems, desires, crisis, issues and needs all become crystallized. Parents can help their children accept any dream they might have by creating an environment where it is safe for children to tell their dreams. No dream is too weird, too confusing, too violent, too sad or too mysterious to be shared. Every dream has something to offer both the dreamer and the ones to whom the dream is told.

When parents demonstrate to their children that they are open to listening to their dreams, not just the "good" ones or the "bad" ones, then children begin to use their own dreams as tools to think through different situations in their lives. This cannot happen if parents hang dream catchers to chase away bad dreams, thereby communicating to their children that bad dreams are destructive and can be made to disappear. There is a reason why a child's unconscious creates each and every dream. If parents try to take a nightmare and change it into a lovely "live happily ever after" dream, they tamper with their child's unconscious.

☁ Every night a young girl woke up from sleep in a state of anxiety. She could not recall any dreams and was unaware that she had dreamt at all. When she was younger she regularly suffered from repeated nightmares and her mother told her not to dream, which replaced the nightmares with anxiety and sleeplessness.

☁ A self-sacrificing teenager dreamt of a bunch of kids swimming in a pool. She reported a nice feeling and added, "I didn't want to wake up. I knew I was dreaming." Knowing that she was dreaming indicated that she was an observer in life, rather than a participant.

☁ A self-conscious teenager dreamt of a deranged man jumping out of the dark. The thought in the dream was: "This is only a dream!" which ended the dream. The conscious pause in the dream limited the teenager's creativity both in the dream and in wakefulness.

When does this relationship between sleep and dreaming begin? Dreaming begins before children are even able to talk. Infants dream. Researchers have documented that infants spend about 50% of their sleep time every day in REM. The other 50%

is spent in no-REM sleep, or quiet sleep. As the infant matures, he will learn to sleep for a prolonged period of time without interruption. Eventually, he will start sleeping and waking at the same time everyday, much to the delight of sleep-deprived parents who may have lost anywhere from 400 to 750 hours of sleep in baby's first year!

But what about those babies who experience prolonged sleep disturbances? It is possible, according to some child development authorities, that infants have "wordless nightmares," which interrupt their sleep. It is impossible to know exactly what infants are responding to in the environment.

The most immediate "environment" is the child's physical self (hunger, physical discomfort, fatigue, etc.), and it is often the physical self which impedes sleep, thus effecting how and what children dream.

Are overtired children creating unpleasant situations during the day because they are recuperating from the previous night's bad dreams? Alternatively, do they have bad dreams at night because of what they have experienced during the day? Which comes first? Both? Neither? Nobody wins.

Although nightmares decrease in frequency for elementary school children, they do tend to have at least one nightmare a week. These dreams and nightmares contain the people and problems which the child is experiencing at the time.

Dreams give the child a place to express his hidden feelings and problems. More than likely, he will have nightmares until the stresses and traumas in his life have either been reconciled or removed. The predominant feeling and struggle which he is experiencing in his dreams and therefore in life, causes the child to be deprived of sleep.

Sleep disturbances and nightmares or bizarre dreams may be indicators to parents and other concerned adults that something might be wrong, even if there is no obvious stress in the child's life.

When children enter adolescence, they begin a whole new phase of life. Not since they were infants have they undergone such acute changes in body, mind, and spirit.

Children between the ages of eight and twelve need at least nine to ten hours sleep a night. During the preteen years, sleep becomes increasingly important.

The consequences of not getting enough sleep and therefore, REM sleep, affects teens just as it does young children and adults. Deprived of their valuable REM sleep, these young people do not have the opportunity to sort through the day's experiences in their dreams. This can, and often does, result in instability in teens.

Taken to extreme, teens might show signs of antisocial behavior. Any factor that might help stabilize a teen's behavior should be given serious consideration. Clearly, a good night's sleep which allows for adequate dream sleep is not something to be taken lightly.

VIII
Speak Up!

Just like sleep talking (somniloquence) screaming in his sleep while having a nightmare is an aggressive act toward others in the household, often by a child who is normally passive when awake. Which raises interesting questions: Is the unconscious aware that there is someone near enough to overhear the dreamer talking out loud in his sleep? The unconscious gives the dreamer words in his dream to tell to the person who needs to hear them. Will the dreamer only speak out if there is someone in particular within earshot? Will he only physically lash out if someone is within reach? A child who speaks while sleeping may not speak clearly. He may laugh, cry, moan, grunt or make other kinds of sounds.

Although a child's uttered words as well as screaming or crying while asleep are part of a dream, the parents' unconscious may hear the words and sounds as though they are directed at them, and rightfully so, for the unconscious attempts to express its concerns directly during sleep to those within earshot.

☁ A young boy who disliked his neighbors for repeatedly complaining that he was too noisy, one night was awakened by his parents who had heard him yell in his sleep. In fact, he yelled loud enough, for the neighbors to hear him – an aggressive act and an affront to the neighbors!

☁ A girl who was resentful that her older sister was not helpful with the care of their baby brother dreamt that he was in danger. In the dream, she tried to hand the baby to someone and called out loud, "Take the baby!" which awakened her sister. These were words she wanted to say to her sister in daytime but didn't, and the dream provided her with the words.

A couple communicated hostility to each other during sleep with language spoken out loud while dreaming. The man, miserly and requiring help with every task (his essence), yelled "Help!" in his sleep, startling his wife who "helped" by waking him up from his nightmare. His wife, who was unable to find a safe outlet for the expression of her negative feelings about his miserly ways, was confronted one morning by her husband who handed her a piece of paper on which he had written down words she had uttered in her sleep: "I don't care if this is the most expensive ice cream in the universe. You go to hell!" Her unconscious used the safety of dreaming to utter those words.

A six-year-old boy shouted out in his sleep, "But I didn't mean to!" waking up his older brother, with whom he shared a room. His brother inquired, "What didn't you mean to?" While the six-year-old did not have an answer, he induced concern in those within earshot.

A man who feared his wife was deceptive, dreamt he tried to look into a car to establish who was seated in the front seat. He noticed that the windshield was foggy and asked out loud in his sleep, "Who are you?" words he did not permit himself to ask his wife in daytime.

A young girl spoke out loud in her sleep, "I wanted to ask you for help, but I knew you wouldn't help me," words she was reluctant to say directly to her parents.

A timid woman who rarely raised her voice, suffered from recurring nightmares accompanied by screams which terrorized her family. Screaming in her sleep was a safe avenue of releasing aggression at the people in her household without culpability, while soliciting concern from those who were within earshot.

In dreams, the unconscious gives the dreamer the freedom to express what he won't allow himself to express in wakefulness. Dreams "give" the dreamer words to say out loud to the person he believes needs to hear them. If the dreamer's words are either hurtful or blaming, the dreamer doesn't have to take responsibility for them. After all he was asleep!

IX
Catch My Dream!

Early in their elementary school career, most children will be introduced to some of the rich history and traditions of Native Americans. In that unit of study is literature including poetry, myths, and legends that are associated with various tribes. One of the most popular legends and one that has great appeal for teachers and students alike is the legend of the Dream Catcher.

Teachers use the legend as a springboard not only for discussion but also for a hands-on project: creating dream catchers. While each dream catcher is unique, there is a fairly universal method in the make. Each element in the dream catcher has particular, if not exact, significance.

The children bend twigs of willow branches or something close to it, into a circle. Not only are the willow's branches flexible, in Europe the willow tree is believed to have healing powers. The children weave yarn around the circular frame until they have created a "web". Then they add feathers to the dream catcher. (Purists will be sure to use eagle's feathers because it is an eagle that appears in the myth.) A variation on the project may include having the children string turquoise or other brightly colored beads on the yarn, solely for decoration. Once the project is completed, the children take it home to do its "work".

For some youngsters, the dream catcher is just another thing that they did at school that day. It is tacked up on the family corkboard next to the phone tree, other drawings and random announcements about sports and school.

Other children take the dream catcher much more seriously. They hang it close to their beds or even tie it to the planks of the top bunk overhead. They know what the dream catcher is supposed to do. And they want it to work.

What exactly is the dream catcher supposed to do? One of the several legends explains the origin of the dream catcher this way:

> Grandmother Spider, who sang the Universe into being, was deeply distressed by the fact that humans were having bad dreams. So she went to the willow tree and asked for a beautiful branch. And she went to the eagle and asked for a powerful feather. Then she bent the branch of the willow into a circle joining all the people of the world. Next, she spun a web of wisdom around the willow branch to catch her children's bad dreams. In the morning, Grandfather Sun's rays burned away all the bad dreams that were caught in the web.

According to Native American beliefs, the air is filled with both good and bad dreams, which have the potential to reach the dreamer. According to the Anishnabe tribe, the beads and feathers on the dream catcher actually caught the good dreams for the dreamer. Other legends relate that the hole in the center of the web allowed good dreams through while bad dreams were trapped in the web until they disappeared in the morning sun. The Washoe Native Indians believe that the dream catcher's hoop guarantees a good night sleep because it will not allow bad dreams to filter through its web. Historically, people thought nightmares were evil spirits or ghosts that took possession of a sleeping body. Tribes such as the Ute of North America relied on specially trained dream doctors to exorcise the evil spirits. In other cultures, such as the Iroquois people, anticipating the dreamers' dreams was the only means to avoid evil befalling you.

People across cultures and across time have feared nightmares. Charms and amulets have been developed to help ward off the bad and induce a good night's sleep. In Japan, for example, people carry *Baku*, small sculptures in the form of a mystical animal. The person who owns the Baku rubs it before going to sleep. He is then blessed with beautiful dreams. If he has bad dreams, he must call the animal's name and the creature will immediately eat the nightmares.

Catch My Dream!

What is a nightmare? Where do they come from? Who has them? These are questions that have concerned people of all ages throughout time. Most nightmares occur during REM sleep, and they usually happen in the latter part of the night's sleep, in the early morning. Studies show that most children have nightmares; it seems to be a part of growing up. If our dreams show us what we are feeling and struggling with in our lives, then it makes sense that people of all ages would experience dreams that contain painful or frightening images. It follows, too, that what seems terrifying for one child would not necessarily scare another child.

Studies also show that some nightmares tend not only to repeat and to intensify, but also to cause problematic behavior during the dreamer's waking hours. This makes sense because until the dreamer understands the problem his nightmare holds and deals with that problem, his behavior will grow worse. His nightmares will intensify, clamoring for attention like a neglected child.

Bad dreams make bad sleep. Not realizing that their children's bad dreams contain important messages, which need to be expressed and explored, parents take extreme measures to try to induce a good night's sleep. Think for a moment about what you do or may have done to calm your child's fears when he has had a nightmare and is afraid of falling back to sleep:

Have you hung a dream catcher somewhere in his room to snare the nightmares in his web and keep him safe until morning?

Many dream theorists suggest that children benefit from embracing the nightmare, becoming a part of it, and rewriting the events and the conclusion. If nightmares are an expression of the dreamer's unconscious feelings, how can the dreamer consciously know how and what to rewrite?

How can we help our children get the rest that they need *without* telling them what to dream? Perhaps the first step is to make our children aware of the importance of sleep, not just from the physical standpoint, but also from a success oriented standpoint. We can help our children understand sleep as a place where they can go to replenish their bodies and their minds.

There really are no bad dreams; it is all in the way that you look at them. In the dream catcher legend, the bad dreams were turned into morning dew that trickled down the length of the eagle's feather and were given back to the earth. The "bad" thing was transformed into something good and nourishing. The same process can take place with our own dreams. When we start attentively listening to our children's dreams and the message that they hold, we will appreciate all that dreams have to offer us.

A young girl told her mother she dreamt about her. In the dream, blood was gushing from her head and her mother did nothing to help. Hearing the dream, the mother asked, "Why don't you dream nice dreams about me?" to which the daughter replied, "Why don't you make nice visits to my dreams?" once more putting the onus on the mother, holding her accountable for her "role" in the dream. Any person cast in a dream is "responsible" for his appearance, behavior and script in the dream, because that person is a problem to the dreamer in daytime.

When the child reaches kindergarten, a new phenomenon often occurs: sleep disorders. These can include nightmares, sleep terrors, sleep walking, calling out in sleep, bedwetting, waking up crying and difficulty falling asleep. This is a developmental period characterized by "separation anxiety'. Bedtime means separation, so children do everything they can to stay awake and to prevent separation.

A number of studies have shown that children who do not get enough sleep lack essential learning skills such as problem-solving, memory and concentration. Teenagers lacking sleep will show a noticeable decline in their academic performance.

X
Doctor Dreams

Signals from the body's cells received by the unconscious mind, as revealed in dreams, when decoded, could yield information vital to the person's physical welfare. The conscious mind, however, is most often unequipped to recognize such clues, thus disregarding danger signals emitted from the unconscious in dreams and slips of the tongue.

Women are known to dream of being pregnant and to dream about the sex of their child before they consciously know that they are pregnant. Both frightening and reassuring, the concept that a dream can help diagnose a medical condition before physical symptoms are recognized by the medical profession, is a field laden with promise.

Dreams reveal many things. They reveal the emotional problems and issues that a person is most bothered by. They put on the "screen" those people who disturb the dreamer in everyday life, along with places and things that are troublesome. The unconscious identifies health conditions and passes this information through dreams.

The connection between the physical body and the unconscious mind has been made long before the 20th century. In China, dreams have been used as clues to illness for thousands of years. *The Yellow Emperor Classic of Internal Medicine*, which is believed to have been written around 1,000 BC, dedicates a section to dreams and illness. The ancient civilizations of both Greece and Egypt also believed in the relationship between the body and the mind. Those ancient civilizations used dreams to heal illness. In fact, Ancient Greece produced one of the most famous healers in history, Asclepius. Often identified as demi-god, Asclepius came to symbolize healing throughout the centuries. His serpent-entwined staff looks remarkably like the caduceus, the symbol of the medical profession. People who needed to be healed would take part in Asclepian dream therapy during which they would sleep in temples waiting to have a dream, which would forecast recovery. Stories of miraculous recovery for the blind, the deaf, the barren, the impotent and many other illnesses are associated with Asclepius' technique.

Among those trained in the Asclepian technique were Hippocrates (c. 460 – 357 BC), Plato (c. 428 – 348 BC) and Aristotle (c. 384 – 322 BC). Hippocrates, the "father of modern medicine," used dreams to diagnose illness. He, and many other Greek philosophers, treated his patients according to their dreams, which highlighted their illnesses. Plato went further than either Asclepius or Hippocrates into the relationship between dreams and the individual's mental and physical life. Not only did he believe that dreams informed the dreamer about his mind and his body, Plato believed that dreams could instruct the dreamer how to proceed in his life.

Aristotle clarified Asclepius' technique. He believed that emotions had to be accompanied by dream images or they would not function correctly. The images created change in the body, bringing about both the illness and its cure. The idea that people should listen to their dreams was not even up for discussion with Aristotle, who wrote, "Even scientific physicians tell us that one should pay diligent attention to dreams ..."

Asclepian dream therapy surfaced under the guise of Christianity in the 3rd century AD. Saints Cosmos and Damian, who were martyred in 278 AD, worked relentlessly to cure the sick. Using techniques derived from Asclepius' sleep therapy, they would facilitate the sleep, which enabled their patients to dream. Using the diagnostic information made available through the dreams, the healers would then administer what they believed was the appropriate cure.

Across time and cultures, dreams have been considered a source of knowledge and wisdom. Shamans, or healers, in many cul-

Doctor Dreams

tures have used dreams to diagnose illness. Native American culture is steeped in beliefs regarding dreams. Though each tribe develops its own understanding of the relationship between the internal and external environment, dreams are generally thought to be an invaluable and reliable source of information, especially regarding healing.

The beginning of the 20th century saw a renewed interest in dreams and dream interpretation. While Freud developed his theory of the id, ego and super ego and Jung revealed the collective unconscious, psychic Edgar Cayce focused on the subconscious as a source of remarkable insights about our physical as well as emotional and mental health. Cayce saw that dreams can help diagnose disease, as well as highlight thoughts and emotions we have avoided. He said, "Dreams are given to us for our benefit. We gain insights about our life."

Some of the dreams which interested Cayce, were dreams that came before an illness actually manifested itself in the dreamer's body. Like the Greeks so many thousands of years before him, Cayce believed that the unconscious was linked to the body so that it was able to become aware of symptoms long before they ever became apparent to the individual. The unconscious tries to communicate this information to the individual through the dream, but the conscious frequently is unable to make the connection of vital information from the unconscious via dreams and the effort and "secrets" are wasted.

Cayce differed from earlier theorists because he believed that the individual, not the psychoanalyst, was the best interpreter of his dream. Which brings us to the matter of interpreting a dream. How can we determine if there is a health "warning" hidden in our dreams? How can we use our children's dreams to help us understand if they are sick? When a child has blatant symptoms such as high fever, vomiting, a croup-like cough and so forth, it is easy to determine that he should see a pediatrician, but what about symptoms that are not so blatant? Other illnesses go undetected until they reach a crisis state. Suddenly both parent and child find themselves rushed off to the emergency room for a ruptured appendix or thrust into a series of tests that reveal advanced disease. Of course, these are extreme examples, but by studying their child's dreams parents may pick up clues that lead them toward a better understanding of their child's physical health.

The dream story will not present the problem in the exact images or language of everyday life; it will disguise the problem. However, the predominant feeling and thought will remain. The key to using dreams as tools in identifying health problems is, again, to ask, "How did you feel in the dream?"; "What were you thinking in the dream?"; and "What connections do you see to your life?" If the dreamer is willing and able to do this work, then valuable information may be gained. The dreamer must do the interpreting, however, because the images and feelings in the dream stem from the dreamer's unconscious. If the parent becomes concerned by the child's dream or the child's interpretation of his dream, the parent schedules a consultation with a physician.

How will the dreamer know if a dream could be about an illness? The more the dreamer pays attention to his dreams, the more parents listen to their child's dreams the more they will learn what their child's essence is, and the better chance they will have of identifying that dream which stands out as the warning dream, the dream which says, "Listen to me! I have something important to say!"

The process of using dreams as medically diagnostic tools is *not* different from using dreams to identify emotional problems and struggles. The unconscious has links to the physical and emotional aspects of the dreamer's life. The task of the mind, both the conscious and the unconscious, is to keep a person alive. The unconscious receives clues about the body's well being, which the conscious may ignore. Whenever there is a significant physical, or emotional problem – the unconscious may create a dream story to bring that problem to center stage.

Doctor Dreams

A girl struggling to lose weight without success dreamt she had joined her friend in crossing a treacherous bridge. Midway the bridge became more difficult to cross and they crawled on their hands and knees over the narrow planks. The girl announced, "I can't do it," as her friend continued crossing the bridge. The language of the dream betrayed her unconscious awareness of the poor prognosis of her ability to lose weight.

A man awakened from a dream hearing himself say, "Something is drastically wrong with me." He could not decide if that meant that there was something actually physically wrong with him or that it pointed to an overwhelming feeling that something was wrong. In the dream, he went into a dirty bathroom as a foreigner walked by. The dreamer was frightened that a "foreign body" had entered his space. After a complete check-up he was reassured that the dream spelled out an emotional problem, namely *fear* of being sick.

XI
Dreams in Psychoanalytic Treatment

The dream thought and language reported to the analyst often include transference communications about the patient-analyst relationship. The analyst studies countertransference (the sum total of the analyst's reactions and attitudes toward the patient) issues raised by the patient's dreams to understand what problem may exist in the treatment and what the analyst's contribution to that problem may be.

The analyst uses intuition and instinct along with studying the patient's associations, to filter the predominant thought and feeling in the dream. A patient unable or unwilling to say something in analysis may dream it. Everything said in a session is an association connected to a dream reported in the session. If the dream is reported in the beginning of the session it makes it easier for the analyst to understand the rest of the material reported in the session. If the dream is presented at the end of the session, it is not as helpful to the analyst to understand the dream associations in the session.

Reporting anger in a dream is a forerunner to the resolution of the resistance (difficulty) to verbalizing direct anger at the analyst. Saying everything in the analytical treatment puts a patient in seeming jeopardy, vulnerable to the analyst's reactions. Not saying everything keeps the patient from getting better. Eventually the patient will say his negative feelings without resorting to language from a dream.

When the patient's dream depicts the analyst doing something wrong or out of character, the analyst studies ways in which he is mishandling the treatment. In fact, whenever the analyst appears in a patient's dream there is a problem in the treatment.

☁ A young actor reported a dream where his father asked about his audition, to which the actor replied, "I don't want to talk about it." In a second dream his agent showed no empathy, and his thought in the dream was, "I want a reaction and I'm not going to get one. It's not working out." The analyst heard the language of the two dreams as transference communications about the treatment.

☁ A man reported a dream of three innocent guys about to be attacked by a gang. In the dream he tried first to call 911 and then accosted a policeman demanding, "I need help now!" That sentence was heard by the analyst as a plea for help in the analytic treatment.

☁ A patient may use a dream to free-associate hostility to the analyst. A middle-aged musician dreamt he asked Paul McCartney to play the guitar. Free-associating, he said that Paul McCartney was not a "deep talent" and added that Mozart as well, "was not a deep talent." The analyst, a Mozart lover, her sensibilities offended, concluded the patient reported a dream as a spring-board to free-associate a hostile communication to the analyst.

☁ A woman who suspected her husband had kept a secret from her throughout their marriage reported a dream describing the scenario in this language: "I knew where he was, but I did not know where he was. I would have been hurt to know where he was. I did not care to know where he was."

Consumed by jealousy, she did not want to know whatever she suspected, and used the dream to give a warning to the analyst that she did not want to know if there was a secret in her marriage.

☁ A jealous young woman who developed manipulative survival techniques, dreamt that an actress, who was a therapy group member, who in life was beautiful and successful, had become homely and was auditioning for a demeaning part. The dream, when reported to the group, provided the dreamer with a safe avenue of attacking the actress free of reprisals.

A patient repeatedly reported sexually perverse and sadistic material claiming that it happened to her in the womb and in infancy, inducing repugnance in the analyst who could hardly listen to the material. The patient, unconsciously aware of the analyst's reaction, began to report the images as dreams. It was not clear if she simply reported her "memories" and called them dreams, or whether she actually dreamt them. The patient's manipulative stance and veracity was put into question. Although the analyst was still engulfed by the sadistic images, she was able to tolerate the material because the patient identified them as dreams and not memories. Outrageous material reported as memories induced temporary feelings of disorientation in the analyst, whereas disconnected and disturbing images reported as dreams were acceptable and tolerated.

A young woman dreamt she was about to purchase a pair of earrings. Realizing that they were a part of a set that included a necklace and a bracelet, she opted to secretly remove the earrings from the set. In life, she secretly tried to separate her boyfriend from his family.

A middle-aged man frustrated by recent bad advice he had received from his psychoanalyst dreamt of telephoning a veterinarian to ask for advice regarding his bleeding cat. In the dream the vet said, "I'll put the cat to sleep," to which the man responded, "But she might live!" The feeling was frustration at receiving incompetent medical advice.

A woman dreamt, her analyst handed her a bill on which was written: "eight sessions and one emerg." Abbreviating the word "emergency" in her dream she pointed out was her feeling that the analyst did not spell things out.

XII
Essence

Take any substance and reduce it to its most fundamental element and you have that object's essence. Everything has a core, a heart and a center, that quintessential part that distinguishes one human being so radically from another is called the essence.

An individual's essence is as enduring and indelible as DNA, in fact, it can be seen as the "DNA of the psyche". It is as unique as a fingerprint; it marks us for life as distinct from every other human being whoever walked, is walking, or will walk on this planet. Although seemingly similar to others' essences, it has its own "variations on a theme" which makes it unique.

The essence is not always altruistic or attractive; however, it is a prevailing driving force, determined by both genes and upbringing. It can be self-serving, such as in pursuit of self-centered goals, or it can be altruistic and self-sacrificing. It is designed to preserve the person both physically and psychologically, while ensuring the person's life will be meaningful to him.

The essence is both a provider and a protector. It gives the individual a reason to live, which could be a "calling" or an ambitious pursuit. At some point in his adult life, a person must think long and hard to bring to consciousness an awareness of what his essence is. In maturing, the individual comes to know his essence, which has become more defined and developed with the passage of time. It is also difficult for an observer to identify another's essence since it is basically the owner's well-kept "secret".

The feelings, thoughts and language of dreams are clues to both the person's unconscious mind and to the way in which he relates to the world, his essence. The individual's essence influences every area of his life, both sleeping and awake. During the day, it shows itself in slips of the tongue and fantasies, and at night, it reveals itself in dreams.

The essence begins to be formed early in life and evolves as the years go by, with clues, and hints appearing both in daytime and in dreams. In the end, the essence as well succumbs to the mortality of man, and appears in the person's last uttered words. Even if one has gone through life in the dark about what his essence is, final words reveal his essence when, at that moment, the unconscious has its say.

Consider some of these final words which tell something of the essence of celebrated characters from history: "One of us must go," Oscar Wilde of the wallpaper in the room where he was dying; "Thank God I have done my duty," Lord Nelson at the Battle of Trafalgar; "So little done, so much to do," Cecil Rhodes; "I'm tired, and I have to go to sleep," Allen Ginsberg; "Well, I've had a happy life," William Hazlitt.

In the final memorial service mourners unknowingly speak of the person's essence.

Our dreams tell us many things. Though the feelings, thoughts, and language of dreams change during the course of a lifetime, there is a tight thread running through dreams, weaving them together into a tapestry which depicts the dreamer's single most significant ambition, which defines his life: his essence.

When the individual's essence is revealed through his dreams, then that person's most significant desire, what lies at the person's "deep heart's core" as the poet W. B. Yeats said, is made known. Generally, we go through our lives interacting with others without knowing what it is that makes them "tick." It is likely that they don't know either what makes them "tick". However, occasionally we meet someone who has worked long and hard to bring to consciousness an awareness of what his essence is.

A performer achieved success and notoriety by surrounding himself with talented people. He presented himself as a great

Essence 77

talent when, in fact, he was using the brains, arms and talent of others – his essence. His entourage remained at his beck and call because of their need for money, which was accompanied by a "promise" of garnering accolades, which never happened. One person who became aware of the performer's essence of using people became disenchanted and left, causing the performer's near failure, as the two essences worked one against the other.

Not discovering our essence is a loss. Shakespeare wrote in *Hamlet*: "This above all, to thine own self be true." Being true to ourselves is a task that requires effort on our parts to understand who we are and why we think, act and feel the way we do. One of the greatest clues to our thoughts and feelings are our dreams. It is in our dreams that we get to the heart of who we are.

"The unexamined life is not worth living," wrote Socrates sometimes around 800 BC. Perhaps what Socrates knew, what Shakespeare knew, what so many great philosophers, writers, thinkers, people throughout history have known is that only when we discover who and what we are, only when we take that information and use it to further our own development, will our lives have meaning. Our dreams provide us with important clues to examine our lives and develop insight into the way in which we function in the world, identifying the deep desire, longing, and determination we harbor in our hearts (often kept secret) – our essence.

The mind, particularly the unconscious mind, is intricately woven and complicated. The main task of the mind, both conscious and unconscious, is to keep the body alive. When destructive elements exist in the mind and gaps in vigilance occur, the unconscious can no longer overcome the onslaught of danger. The unconscious, when ignored or disrespected, forfeits exploring danger signals in dreams and slips of the tongue. The conscious, too often, is inept in decoding signals emitted by the unconscious.

A person's every breath, every move and every dream involves his essence, which builds a protective shield over the mass of cells which constitutes the human being.

💭 A millionairess dreamt that she went to the supermarket to buy milk in big quantity to save money. Her essence was stinginess.

💭 A young girl was chronically late for school. She did everything a little late – which was her essence. When she was born, her mother's gynecologist had, for his own convenience, induced labor prior to the due date. This seemed to have mobilized in the young girl the need to postpone everything. Her essence repeatedly attempted to catch up with her "rightful" due date.

💭 A teenager whose essence was preoccupation with unimportant details dreamt he ate human flesh. His concern in the dream was trying to figure out whether it was the flesh of a man or a woman, which duplicated his essence of preoccupation with irrelevant detail.

💭 A girl, whose essence was pining to walk with royalty, dreamt that Bill Clinton and she were walking together through crowds.

💭 A young girl's essence was her need for proof of every occurrence, dreamt that two cats were fighting. Despite noting the severe bite marks, limping paws and blood, her thought in the dream was uncertainty that the cats were really hurt.

XIII
Once Upon a Dream

Children's literature is full of books that describe fictional characters who struggle with problems, feelings and fears in their dreams. In fact, some of the best loved children's books are built on such dreams: Maurice Sandak's *Where the Wild Things Are* is the story of Max, a preschooler who acts like such a monster that he is sent to bed without supper. He falls asleep and dreams of sailing away to an island where he is King of the Wild Things. But he grows lonely and bored and wants to return home, which he does. When he wakes up dinner is still warm.

Jean de Brunhoff's *Babar the King* contains an interesting dream. Unlike Max's dream, which Max appears to have initially enjoyed, Babar's dream is more of a nightmare with a happy ending. In his dream, Babar sees that the day has begun well for Celestville. Flowers bloom, children sing, tennis players play tennis, sailboats sail on the smooth lake. But then, suddenly, a snake bites Babar's dear friend the Old Lady and she falls quite ill. Then, a fire breaks out in Babar's close advisor Cornelius' house and almost suffocates him. That night Babar dreams of ugly monsters named "Anger", "Stupidity", "Fear", and "Sickness" flying toward him. Then suddenly they are chased away by beautiful winged elephants named "Hope", "Joy", "Courage", "Learning", "Work", and "Patience". When "he woke, he felt ever so much better."

Famous dream stories include Frank Baum's *Oz* stories, which take place during a dream, E.T.A. Hoffman's *The Nutcracker* and Charles Dickens' *A Christmas Carol*. There are many variations of Hoffman's story, but in all of them Clara dreams of the battle between the Mouse King and the Nutcracker. After the Mouse King has been slain, she and the Nutcracker travel to a marvelous land full of sugarplums, marzipan and other delicacies.

Her experience is so real that she does not believe that it was a dream at all; however, the events are so fantastic, they could never have taken place in real life.

One of the places that the four young people in the *Dawn Treader* encounter along the way is a place "that was not land at all, nor even, in an ordinary sense, a mist. It was a Darkness." The young men and women are ready to turn around, but Reepicheep, their rat companion, urges them on. "I hope it will never be told in Narnia," he says, "that a company of noble and royal persons in the flower of their age turned tail because they were afraid of the dark." And so, they go on.

Everything about this place is desolate and very cold. Time seems to have lost it's meaning and the journey into the darkness goes on forever. Suddenly, the lonely, black cold is split by a bloodcurdling cry: "Even if you are only one more dream, have mercy! Do not fade away and leave me in this horrible land." The voice belongs to a gaunt, ravaged man whom they take aboard. The man's most noticeable features are his eyes – opened as wide and round as they could be; they reflect both agony and horror. "Fly! Fly! Row for your lives away from this accursed shore!" he cries.

There are many books and poems that involve dreams as their core, for we spend almost half our life sleeping and much of that time dreaming.

On the back cover of one edition of *The Voyage of the Dawn Treader* Book 5 in C. S. Lewis' *The Chronicles of Narnia*, is the inscription: "The Dawn Treader will take you places you never dreamed existed." In the book, the quartet of young travelers journey further than they have ever gone before as they sail toward the country at the End of the World. Much of what they see and experience they never would have imagined except in their dreams because dreams allow the unimaginable to happen. In dreams, magic rules and reason makes way for wonder, awe and fear.

Luckily, for characters and reader alike, an albatross comes to their rescue and they find themselves out of the Darkness and into the sunlit world once more. The danger has passed. For the reader, however, there will be no heroic albatross to rescue him. He must free himself from his own nightmares by coming to terms with the issues and problems that are represented in his dream story.

The notion presented by Reepicheep that being afraid of the dark requires sailing into not running away from the fear. Those things, which are troublesome to us in our everyday life, will surface in our dreams; therefore, it is important to face fears squarely on rather than try to elude them.

Max's dream shows a little boy who wants very much to express his wild feelings and to be exulted for them. It shows a little boy who wants to have the power and authority that no young child experiences. It also shows a little boy who longs for the safety, security and familiarity of home. Max's problem is one of reconciling his wild side with the Max who must live in society and behave according to society's rules.

Dorothy's adventures in *The Wizard of Oz* seem to her so real that, when she wakes, she is convinced that the people who appeared in her dream were actually with her. This phenomenon makes dreams both fascinating and disturbing to children. Children are drawn to the dream's ability to seem so real. They are also repelled by this, because what appears in dreams is not always what we want to see. For example, Dorothy regrets having run away and that she wants to be back home with her family. The whole dream story is based on the notion that "there's no place like home." Everything in her dream relates to the problem of getting home. So how do the other situations and characters fit in? They are people with whom Dorothy has a problem. They are, somehow involved in the greater problem of the dream.

Dreams like this and like Charles Dickens' *A Christmas Carol*, show the dreamer his most immediate concerns. The unconscious plays out for the dreamer how things might turn out should the dreamer not take the "right" path. The feelings in dreams such as these, are so acute that the dreamer is propelled into action. When feelings are so strong and dreams are so clear, the dreamer must be grappling with a significant problem.

In the book about the little child, who sees himself in Plunk, he knows that his dreams allow him to be someone different, to be more adventurous or courageous than he normally feels. He knows, too, that he wakes in the morning and carries those dream feelings with him. If he has a nightmare, he may feel scared throughout the day, just like Plunk. If he has a happy dream in which he feels strong and in control, those feelings of empowerment will go with him in his everyday life. Reading about a character like Plunk allows the child to identify and to embrace his own experience with his dreams.

XIV
Pharaoh's Man

Children are curious. They want to know about the origin of everything. They ask their parents, "Where do babies comes from?"; "Why do we have seasons?"; "Who made the Sun? The moon? The stars?" It is therefore not surprising that they are curious about dreams.

In Ancient Egypt, shamans, the world's first psychoanalysts interpreted dreams as an integral part of their healing practices. The Old Testament story of Jacob's dream at Bethel was written sometime between 800 and 500 BC:

> He dreamed that there was a ladder set upon the earth, and the top of it reached to heaven; and behold, the angels of God were ascending and descending on it!

Jacob's youngest son Joseph had many dreams which changed the course of his life. There was one in which Joseph's sheaf of wheat had the eleven other sheaves (his brothers) bow down before him. For that dream, Joseph's brothers threw him into a pit. When his gift as an interpreter of dreams was discovered, he was elevated in rank until he became Pharaoh's right-hand man.

As early as 350 BC, the Greek philosopher Aristotle was investigating dreams. This was significant especially because in his culture many people "assumed that in sleep a neighbor neither sees, nor hears, nor exercises any sense whatever." Aristotle went on to show that in dreaming we do use our senses. Many of his observations were similar to those of modern scientists.

From Aristotle on for the next thousand years or so, dreams were generally accepted as a reality, although they were understood in diverse ways. In his classic study *The Golden Bough*, J. G. Frazer recounts a belief common to the Indians of both Brazil and Guinea: When a person is sleeping, his "soul is supposed to wander away from his body and actually visit the places, to see the persons and to perform the acts of which he dreams."

People throughout time have believed that dreams were prophecies, messages from the divine. Jacob's dream mentioned previously is an example of this. They have also seen bad dreams or nightmares as visits from evil spirits.

It wasn't until the middle of the nineteenth century that a radically new way of understanding dreams emerged. The person who revolutionized dream interpretation was the Moravian psychoanalyst Sigmund Freud.

Perhaps you have had an experience similar to this: A rather unpleasant aunt comes to visit. When you open the door, you greet her saying: "Hello Aunt Rat!" instead of "Aunt Pat". According to Freud, slips of the tongue like this, obsessive behaviors like ferocious teeth grinding, and dreams all result from mental processes over which we have no control.

While analyzing patients' dreams, Freud distinguished between what the dream seemed to be about and what the dream was about. Dreams, according to Freud's then radical new theory, are the dreamer's repressed desires. He called dreams a "safety valve" for these unconscious longings. When a Freudian analyst interprets a dream, he should be able to zero in on the repressed desires that are creating the patient's problems and that brought the patient into analysis in the first place.

In 1906, Freud met the Swiss psychiatrist Carl Jung who shared many of Freud's beliefs about the way that the mind functioned. The two worked closely together until 1914. By then, Jung had outgrown Freud's theories. He didn't believe that all neurosis could be traced back to sexual trauma or that the Oedipal complex should be taken literally.

What did Jung believe? He developed his own revolutionary theory of the unconscious in which he proposed that the unconscious consisted of two elements – the personal unconscious and the collective unconscious.

The personal unconscious is all the material that belongs exclusively to the individual. This would include people, places, things and events that have special meaning for the individual. In contrast, the collective unconscious is made up of archetypes or symbols that have universal meaning. Jung believed that symbols in dreams were just that – symbols; he believed that these symbols had a universal meaning that was common to all dreams.

Another major development in dream interpretation occurred in the 1950's. Until this time, most people thought that when we went to sleep, we didn't do anything except sleep. They believed that we lay passive as pillows until we woke in the morning.

Though psychiatrists had been studying dreams since the mid-19th century, scientists had contributed little to the effort. But with the discovery of REM sleep, scientists were spurred on to begin significant studies of sleep and dreaming. What they discovered was fascinating.

Newborns experience REM sleep as soon as they fall asleep. They spend 50% of their sleep time in REM sleep, in contrast to adults who only spend 20% of their sleep time in REM. However, REM sleep in infants does not mean dreaming as it does in adults. Scientists believe that infants' brains need the stimulation of REM sleep because the infants themselves are infrequently alert. But, the baby's brain needs stimulation in order for the central nervous system to develop properly. While the baby sleeps, the brain receives the stimulation it requires. However, that stimulation does not involve dreams and dreaming.

We are quite active participants as we make our way nightly through five phases of sleep: stages 1,2,3,4 and REM sleep. Each stage is unique, like the movements of a symphony. In the first stage, we sleep lightly, drifting in and out of sleep, and we can be woken easily. This is also the stage when both our eye movement and muscle activity are slow. Have you ever experienced the feeling of suddenly jerking awake? This is actually a muscle contraction called *hypnic myoclonia* that is common to this stage.

Stage two occupies about 50% of our total sleep time. Here, our eyes stop moving and our brain waves slow way down. Occasionally, fast brain waves known as *sleep spindles* burst forth. Then, in the third stage, *delta waves*, which are extremely slow brain waves, appear. They are interrupted by waves that are both small and fast. By the time that we reach stage four, our minds are almost exclusively producing delta waves.

Have your children ever experienced bedwetting, night terrors or sleepwalking? These phenomena occur during stage three and four sleep, together called *deep sleep*, because it is so difficult to wake someone from this. Unlike in earlier stages, there is no eye or muscle movement during these stages. If someone is woken, he will be disoriented or groggy. In the morning, he may not even remember what he said or did or that he was woken at all!

Last but most certainly not least comes REM. Our body changes radically when we enter REM. Our breathing becomes fast, shallow and irregular; our eyes snap randomly from side to side, up and down. Our heart rate increases, our blood pressure goes up and males often get penile erections. The only part of our anatomy that seems to lie limp in REM are our limbs which become temporarily paralyzed.

What is so significant about REM? It is during REM that dreams as we think of them, disjointed, fragmented, illusive and unclear, occur. We spend about two hours every night dreaming. You don't need to be a math whiz to know that *most people will have spent tens of thousands of hours dreaming during their lifetime*. Tens of thousands of hours of dreaming means tens of thousands of disjointed, fragmented, illusive, disjoined dreams. While scientists cannot tell us how or why we dream, they can describe REM.

REM sleep starts when a signal from the pons, an area at the base of the brain, makes its way to an area of the brain called the *thalamus*. The thalamus picks up the signal and replays it to the *cerebral cortex*. This is the brain's "command central". It is the outer layer that takes all the information we gather from our environment while we are conscious and organizes it. According to some scientists, when the cortex receives sporadic signals during REM sleep, it tries to make some kind of sense of those signals by creating dreams.

There is also a group of cognitive scientists who believe that dreams have no purpose at all. They argue that since we remember so few of our dreams, how can they be so important?

Dreams have fascinated people for thousands of years. They fascinate us still. In the words of Lewis Carroll's Alice, we grow "curiouser and curiouser" every day.

XV
Dream Scape

Although sleep may be used as an escape from daily worries, in dreams problems are dealt with and, once reported, dreams are not a purely private experience. Dreams often compel the dreamer to share recollected dreams with others. This creates an opportunity for unconscious communication and manipulation.

An expression surfaced sometime in the mid-80's and has been tossed across the culture like a Frisbee: "You can't win if you don't play." Keeping the cadence but changing the words, let's toss out this thought: "You can't dream if you don't sleep." As glib as that sounds, there are very serious ramifications to not sleeping or to having sleep interrupted and, consequently, to have the dream life disturbed. Ask any sleep-deprived parents who are struggling with a newborn that has no sense of boundaries or time. Studies show that after a new baby is born, parents will lose anywhere from 400 to 750 hours of sleep in the first year! But parents may be bringing this sleep deprivation on themselves by not allowing the babies to "self-soothe" before rushing in to pacify them.

It is critical to the infant's well being that he learn to go to sleep in his crib by himself and that he sleep for a prolonged period of time without interruption. If the baby can do this then he has learned how to sleep, a skill which he will need throughout his life.

As soon as a child is born, the contest between sleep and the environment begins. One syndrome which effects infant sleep between the ages of one to three months is *colic*. Anyone who has lived through this experience with an infant will remember the intense, inexplicable, intermittent crying which occurs during the night, usually at the same time in the sleep/wake cycle. While this generally passes once the baby reaches three months, it can cause emotional and psychological stress in the family as well as deprive everyone in the home of much needed sleep.

By the time they are six years old, most children have their circadian rhythms firmly set.

However, when children begin elementary school they experience developmental separation from their parents, and this is often accompanied by headaches, stomachaches, and poor concentration. In the evening, bedtime becomes an ordeal. Once in bed, there are multiple requests for water, kisses, hugs, or any other diversions. When the child is finally asleep, he may experience nightmares, bedwetting, talking in his sleep, teeth grinding, multiple awakenings, or night terrors. These nighttime experiences take place primarily during stage 3/4 sleep – deep sleep when the child is not awake or even aware of what is going on, but his parents are. Their sleep has been interrupted yet again.

Why do children experience sleep disturbances? Many studies from sources throughout the world state this fact: children's sleep is very sensitive to environmental factors. If stresses and traumas such as divorce, death in the family, and a move to a new state are thrown in on top of an already susceptible young person then what will happen to his sleep and his dreams? According to researchers, there is a direct relationship between sleep problems and children's well being. Stress contributes to sleep problems in children and sleep problems exacerbate their stress. Once again, the wheels go round and round.

Sleep disturbances and nightmares or bizarre dreams can be used as warning flags that something might be wrong even if there is no apparent stress in the child's life. If a child chooses to share his dreams, he has a safe place to explore his feelings in the dreams.

Aside from children's schedules and demands, what are other environmental disturbances that might impede sleep either in an adult or in a child? Grief. One of the greatest stresses in anyone's life is losing someone whom you love. Often adults lose sleep after someone close has died, or perhaps find themselves sleeping too much because they are depressed. Sometimes, the deceased appears in a dream.

Like adults, children grieve. Like adults frequently do, they experience sleep disturbances as part of that grief process. They may be afraid to fall asleep because they fear that they will not ever wake up. Or they are afraid of what they will dream.

Children grieve other losses, too: pets dying of old age or those getting run over, losing friends to moves or relatives lost to the whims of age. These are losses that often create feelings, which children cannot express and which end up in their dreams.

On a more objective level, noise interrupts sleep. In the early 90's, one problem that received a lot of publicity was jet noise. People complained that the noise of the planes interfered with their sleep. Research has shown that exposure to any noise while sleeping, if the sleeper doesn't wake up, can stop the immune system from functioning. In addition, unfamiliar noise or noise that we hear during the first and last two hours of sleep, has the most adverse effect on the sleep cycle. This might be a dog barking in the neighborhood, a train tooting its horn as it passes through town, the garbage trucks emptying the dumpsters, or your spouse wheezing beside you. Whatever it is, it's noise.

Light affects dreams. This could be the light of the morning sun pouring through curtains; it could be the yellow green glow of streetlights beyond a hotel window. But it could also be the tiny light that a compact digital clock emits. This miniscule light can disturb the sleep cycle even if it doesn't wake a person up. How? It stops activity in the sleep center of the brain, where sleep chemicals plummet within minutes.

Temperature affects sleep and dreams. It may also be why on a sticky, summer night the dreamer has a dream about warm locations. Or, conversely, if the dreamer is too cold, he may find himself dreaming of a cold place or of being unprotected against the elements. *Whatever the external stimuli, if they are a problem to the dreamer the unconscious will take them and work them into the dream.*

Food affects sleep and dreams. Studies show that a big or rich meal which causes indigestion before bed will keep you up. However, doctors often recommend having a cup of warm soup as an antidote for insomnia. Certain foods are thought to influence dreams, though scientific proof for this is lacking.

Alcohol has a negative effect on both the quality of sleep and the quality of daytime life. Alcohol may induce sleep, but it doesn't take long before it reverses and ruins both the quality and the length and depth of sleep. It turns serene sleep into fragmented sleep and produces either nightmares or insomnia.

Studies have shown that some teenagers need as much sleep as small children – about ten hours a night. However, for the most part, they do not get anywhere near that much sleep. Most teens experience sleep deprivation, a condition which exists if an individual falls asleep in less than five minutes. Ideally, a person falls asleep in ten to fifteen minutes; this indicates that the person is sufficiently tired to fall asleep, but not so exhausted that he has barely made it through the day. But for the most part, they do not get anywhere near that much sleep because of environmental factors such as school, after-school activities, and television.

There are serious ramifications to not sleeping or to having REM sleep interrupted and, consequently, to having the dream life disturbed, for it is during REM sleep that most of our dreams take place. In dreams, the unconscious processes the individual's feelings and struggles.

Children who suffer from sleep/dream deprivation, being awakened at the beginning of REM sleep, and consequently deprived of much of their dream sleep, tend to become disoriented, bad tempered and unstable.

But what about those babies who experience prolonged sleep disturbances? It is possible, according to some authorities in child development, that infants have "wordless nightmares," which interrupt their sleep.

According to the National Institute of Health, about 25 percent of American children between the ages of 1 and 5 have sleep disturbance. Like infants, these preschoolers can and do dream. A two-year-old child is much less able to verbally express his feelings about his world than an eight-year-old child. So where do the feelings of frustration, anxiety, fear and confusion come out? In dreams! Children need undisturbed sleep so that their brains can help the child grow and thrive. Many children are overtired, bad tempered, moody and unfocused. Parents search for causes, answers, remedies – anything to explain and cure this behavior. By the time they are six years old, children are gaining better mastery of their world. However, developmentally children of this age must separate from their parents, a process which often produces anxiety, headaches, stomachaches, poor concentration.

When they do sleep and dream, the factors, which seem to influence teens the most are television and peers. A study conducted by the department of pediatrics at Rhode Island Hospital connected television to significant sleep disturbances including resisting going to bed, having trouble falling asleep, not sleeping as long as usual, having anxiety about sleep, and experiencing daytime sleepiness. Researchers found that the following habits were directly associated with the sleep disturbances: having a television in the child's bedroom, allowing the use of the TV as a sleep aid, and unrestricted amount of TV viewed.

Dreaming depends on who is sleeping next to or near the dreamer. Sounds, smells, and light affect sleep and infiltrate dreams. Unfamiliar noise, or noise that we hear during the first and last two hours of sleep, has the most adverse affect on the sleep cycle because this is a period of active REM sleep and dreaming. Sometimes the noise from the outside environment will not wake the dreamer immediately; first, the unconscious will incorporate the noise into the dream. One couple reported that they were woken by their daughter knocking lightly on their bedroom door. Just before waking, the wife heard a taping sound, like a hammer, in her dream. Any noise that appears in a dream may be related to sounds in the dreamer's environment. Light insinuates itself into dreams. The unconscious often takes the external stimulus of the light and makes it a part of what is going on in the dream.

Summary

Parents can learn a great deal about their children by listening to their dreams. Dreams provide insight into their children's fears, struggles and who troubles them. For a parent this is incredibly important. Imagine being able to find out what is really at the bottom of your child's worries, and what issues your child has, just by listening to his dreams.

Reporting a dream is a safe avenue for expressing thoughts and feelings of which the child is either unaware, unwilling, or unable to communicate directly. Through dreams, the unconscious has license to freely express hostile feelings, circumventing inhibitions. This is a manipulative strategy the unconscious uses to communicate to whom the dream is reported.

Dreams affect behavior and feelings in daytime, providing inertia to solving problems or "paralyzing" the dreamer into inaction when impulsive action would be contraindicated.

The person's recollected dream is like a game of charades, where the dreamer is asked to identify the predominant feeling and thought in the dream, which invariably is the predominant feeling and thought the dreamer struggles with in waking hours.

Sometimes dreamers don't even know what those problems are or how deeply they affect them. But the dreams do, because they are being coached by the unconscious. For this reason, parents can get to know their children's problems by listening to their dreams.

Dreams tell us many things. Though the feelings, thoughts and language of dreams change during the course of a lifetime, there is a thread running through a person's dreams weaving them together into a tapestry which depicts the most significant concern in the dreamer's life which defines his life. That is his essence.

Adults must deal with their own troubling dreams, but doing so is harder for children. They have difficulty sorting out the real from the imaginary. They can awaken from a dream and really believe that the Big Bad Wolf was chasing them, that Mom and Dad left them alone in the park, or that they were falling through space. Some children even fear bedtime because they are afraid they might have "that dream". Every parent is familiar with interrupted sleep, and the figure of a tearful child standing next to the bed, half-awake, relating some preposterous-but terrifying-adventure that "happened" during the night, in the "movie" the child's unconscious created.

Children are too often reassured that there is no monster under the bed. "It was only a dream. Let's take a look ... see! ... just your shoes. Now go back to sleep and have *pleasant* dreams this time. Mom and Dad are not going away, and in any case would never go anywhere without their little darling." And: "There are no wolves around here. Not within a thousand miles! And besides, no wolf could get into our house. Nobody ever is hurt by a wolf. And Dad would show that wolf if it ever tried to hurt you!" And then the parent may try to empower the child with a dream journal. Anything from a $.99 marbleized school notebook to a deluxe velour-covered, black-paged notebook complete with a silver gel pen encouraging the child to write down his dream.

The parent should have listened in silence to the child's dream and then asked him what his feeling was in the dream. The parent in the privacy and silence of his own mind, then searches for what may be going on in his child's life.

Appendix

A New Understanding of Dreams*

Three principles can guide an analyst into a patient's unconscious: dreams reflect the struggle of a patient's immediate life; the patient communicates this struggle in reporting dreams; and the content of dreams are inherently troubling to the dreamer.

To use dreams constructively in psychoanalysis, it is essential to develop an understanding of what is communicated by the dream and the motivation of the dreamer for reporting the dream. This article will review practical aspects of these broad areas of dream interpretation in psychoanalytic practice.

A patient's dreams come into the psychoanalytic dialogue; the patient might ask for some explanation of his dreams, or the analyst instinctively may ask the patient: "What are you dreaming?" This can be useful when the analyst needs clarification of the state of the patient's unconscious mind. Asking for identification of the patient's feeling or thought in a dream often helps the analyst understand the underlying problem that is the source of struggle in the patient's waking hours. The dream reveals the emotion that is of immediate importance in the patient's life.

Rather than trying to determine the "general attitude" of a patient through his dreams, it is more useful to apply the information from a patient's dream to current problems with which the

---

* Article published in **New Jersey Medicine**, the Journal of the Medical Society of New Jersey, Vol. 92, No. 1, Jan. 1995, by **Ruth Velikovsky Sharon**, Ph.D. Reprinted with kind permission of the **Medical Society of New Jersey**.

patient is struggling. Although the story in the dream often is an enigma and difficult to analyze, the feeling, thought, and language of the dream scenario are clues to important issues in the patient's immediate life situation; only in the dream, the cast of characters and situations are different. The predominant feeling and thought in the dream is the predominant feeling and thought the dreamer struggles with in waking hours. As the struggle and predicament in daily life change, so do the feeling and thought in the patient's dreams. The following dream fragment is an example: A woman dreamt her cat faded into a skeleton and she did nothing to prevent it. She identified the feeling of guilt in the dream, which in waking hours she experienced as neglecting her son in favor of a new relationship with a man.

Some dreams seem to be designed to provoke a response in the dreamer, prodding toward new attitudes and actions. The following is an example of self-manipulation in a dream: A young man enraged with a former boss who had fired him expected to see the boss at a formal function. Possessing a protective unconscious, the man experienced a pleasant dream about the former boss the night before the event, leading to the temporary unconscious resolution of the negative feelings toward the employer. Thus, the patient was able to tolerate the social event and behave appropriately.

The predominant feeling with which the patient is struggling in life is heightened and magnified by the dream.

The dream feeling crystallizes the feeling with which the patient is struggling, bringing to consciousness a surge toward resolution of the struggle. It is important to add, however, that if the patient is not yet equipped to solve the immediate problem, and impulsive action would be contraindicated, the dream may have a debilitating effect, contributing to the patient's depressive feelings and emotional paralysis.

Dream Motivation

Dream emotion reflects the dreamer's feeling concerning a real problem or dilemma in the person's life, rather than a wish fulfillment or desirable solution to a problem.

The dreamer has a problem in life with every person, object, and location appearing in the dream, regardless of the positive or negative portrayals in the scenario of the dream. By casting a recognizable person in a dream, the dreamer reveals having a problem with that person in wakefulness, even if the dream scenario does not indicate it. (The principle of disguising negative feelings with positive dream scenarios recently has been described by Gollub as "opposite emotionality".[1])

It is not an honor to be cast in another's dream. People in the dream are involuntary actors, cast because the dreamer has innate anger toward them, thereby placing suspicion on the dreamer's relationship to the person or persons in wakefulness. Whomever and whatever appears in the dream is a problem to the dreamer in wakefulness; this includes representations of the dreamer himself. The dreamer is the camera's eye, elusively participating in each dream. When the dreamer appears visually in the dream – in front of the camera – the dreamer reveals self-hatred in waking hours. The following dream fragment is an example: A man whose hope of becoming a famous actor did not materialize, repeatedly dreamt of famous actors. Seemingly a namedropper, in actuality he disliked the actors he cast in his dreams because of envy. In one dream, he found himself in bed with a famous actor who was making sexual advances toward him. The dream reflected the man's feelings of envy as well as his homophobia.

Unidentifiable people appearing in the dream signal the dreamer's problem with strangers. When the recognizable figure in the dream is deceased, the dreamer's unresolved feelings have followed that person to the grave.

---

[1] Gollub, D.: »A new approach to dream interpretation«, *Psychology* 29 (1992), 39-43.

A recurring dream signals the dreamer's self-perception of lacking creativity in having created the same movie over and over.

The dream thought and language reported to the analyst often include transference communications about the patient-analyst relationship. The analyst studies countertransference issues (the sum total of the analyst's reactions and attitudes toward the patient) raised by the patient's dreams to understand what problem may exist in the treatment and what may be the analyst's contribution to that problem. The image of the analyst in the patient's dream, regardless of the scenario, signals that the patient harbors anger toward the analyst. Analysts have written accounts of patients' dreams depicting the analyst in a negative light, but attribute these portrayals to issues within the patient's personality.[1,2] When the dream depicts the analyst doing something wrong or out of character, however, the analyst should be particularly alerted to study countertransference issues and ways the analyst may be mishandling the treatment.

In one day's work, an analyst heard several patients recount dreams from the previous night in which the analyst appeared. By dreaming about the analyst, the patients, in unison, were sounding an alarm that the analyst was not doing a good job – trying to be in too many places at once.

Patients who are unable or unwilling to say, or who are unaware of what they are feeling about the analyst, may report a dream for the purpose of communicating transference issues (the sum total of the patient's reactions and attitudes toward the analyst), including hostility toward the analyst, without fearing the wrath of the analyst. A patient unable to express anger at the analyst because of fear of retaliation reported a dream in which she yelled at the analyst. In reporting the dream, the patient indirectly attacked the analyst with the dream content, a forerunner to the resolution of the transference resistance to verbalizing the

---

[1] Bonime, W.: »Dreams, insight, and functional change«, *J. Am. Acad. Psychoanalysis* 19 (1991), 124-140.
[2] Glucksman, M.: »The use of successive dreams to facilitate and document change during treatment«, *J. Am. Acad. Psychoanalysis* 16 (1988), 47-70.

anger directly to the analyst. Did she unconsciously create the dream in order to attack the analyst in safety?

Dream language reported to the analyst, taken out of the context of the dream scenario, may be heard by the analyst as communications to the analyst about the analyst. Does a patient manufacture a dream for the purpose of writing into the "script" communications the patient wants to say to the analyst, but is unwilling or unable to verbalize directly? Although the analyst does not appear as a character in the following example, the dream is designed to express language directed toward the analyst, illustrating this principle of communication with the analyst: A young man, raised by a seductive mother, reported a dream in which a salesgirl did not know how to ring up his merchandise. He asked for the manager who in turn called a security guard. Feeling threatened by the situation, the dreamer exclaimed, "You touch me and I'll sue you!" That communication, although in response to dream content, was understood by the analyst as a transference communication.

In addition to using dreams to make indirect transference communications to the analyst, dream reporting can be used to safely manipulate the emotions of other people in the dreamer's life. Once reported, dreams are not a purely private experience. Dreams often compel the dreamer to share recalled dream content with other people. This creates an opportunity for unconscious communication, and raises the following question: Does the unconscious mind create a dream for the purpose of surreptitiously communicating with people to whom the dream will be reported? An example of this phenomenon is: A young woman dreamed she bought a gown for an upcoming occasion. Too shy to ask outright for what she wanted, she reported the dream to a family member who she knew would buy a new gown for her.

Is the unconscious aware that there is someone within earshot to hear the words spoken out loud by the dreamer while dreaming? In the following situation, words spoken out in sleep serve a manipulative purpose: A woman who was resentful that her husband was not helpful in the care of their baby dreamt that her baby was in danger. In the dream she tried to hand the baby to her husband. She yelled, "Take the baby!" out loud in her sleep, which awakened her husband.

Dream Creation

Dreams can be viewed as manipulations, an active ingredient in the dreamer's relational life. The unconscious may form a dream around the need to express a powerful feeling to a particular person in the dreamer's life; the dream itself motivates the dreamer to communicate the dream to that person. The unconscious also attempts to express its concerns directly during sleep to those within earshot of the dreamer's language spoken out during sleep. Through dreams, the unconscious has licence to express hostile feelings freely, circumventing the inhibitions of conscious editing.

Few authors have even approached this idea that dreams are formed to communicate particular ideas to people in the dreamer's life. The predominant view of dreams seems to be that they are formed based on fundamental patterns of the patient's unconscious thought, and these patterns will replay themselves until a substantial change is brought about in the personality of the patient. Any evident "tailoring" of the dream for communication to the analyst has been attributed to "secondary revision", a semiconscious process of editing and adding criticism to a dream that changes how the patient remembers and reports a dream. [1] [2]

I address the role of the unconscious in creating dreams to express the predominant emotions and struggles of the patient. This takes a variety of forms, ranging from a dreamer's speech while asleep to pointed communications to the analyst delivered in the language of a character in a dream.

---

[1] Gillman, R.: »Dreams as resistance« in Rothstein, A.: *The Interpretations of Dreams in Clinical Work*, Madison, CT, International Universities Press (1987).

[2] Stein, M.: »How dreams are told: Secondary revision – the critic, the editor, and the plagiarist«, *J. Am. Psychoanalytic Assoc.* 37 (1989), 65-88.

It is suggested here that, without resorting to an elaborate interpretive system, the following three principles can guide analysts to important insights into a patient's unconscious: dreams reflect or duplicate the feeling of the predominant struggle of the patient's immediate life; the patient communicates these issues in reporting dreams; and the characters, situations, and settings of a dream are inherently troubling to the dreamer.

Conclusions

The dream expresses the patient's feeling relating to a current problem in the patient's life. The analyst uses the patient's dream report to identify the predominant emotion of the struggle in the patient's life, and to understand the patient's resistance to direct verbalization of the thoughts and feelings reflected in the dream reporting.

Reporting a dream is a safe avenue for expressing thoughts and feelings of which the patient is unaware, or is unwilling or is unable to communicate directly. This is a manipulative strategy the unconscious uses to communicate with the analyst, a therapy group, family members, or others to whom the dream is reported. A particular character will be cast in the dream for the purpose of creating the impetus to consciously report the dream content to that person.

Often a patient will recall specific statements or thoughts from a dream which, when removed from the dream context, can be understood as transference communications to the analyst. These statements are particularly useful in helping the analyst study countertransference issues.

In some cases, the feelings of the patient are revealed in vocalization during sleep. Again, this is unconscious manipulative behavior on the part of the dreamer who vents hostility to others in his household.

The emotions experienced during dreams reinforce or amplify the patient's feelings when awake. Dreams affect behavior and feelings in daytime, providing inertia to solving problems or paralyzing the dreamer into inaction when impulsive action would be counterindicated. A dream may provoke action and change attitudes in the face of particularly difficult issues in the patient's life. Such dreams can be seen as self-manipulations, temporarily resolving a conflict.

Ruth Velikovsky Sharon, Ph.D.

Index

(**Hint for the user**: Page numbers with 'f' or 'ff' refer to the following page(s) as well, which usually indicates a more detailed reference to the topic.)

A

adolescence 56
affection 29
AIDS 27
alcohol 92
amulets 62
analyst 47, 71ff, 84, 97, 100ff,
  see also psychoanalyst
anger 18, 29, 39, 42-47, 50, 71,
  79, 99f
animosity 29, 45
anxiety 14, 19, 37, 41f, 50, 54, 93
apnea 37
archetypes 85
Aristotle 66, 83
Asclepius 65f
Athene 43

B

Baku 62
Baum, Frank 79
bedwetting 64, 86, 90
behavior 14, 26, 37, 49, 56, 63f,
  93, 95, 103
brain 44, 85f, 91
Brazil 83
Brunhoff, Jean de 79

C

Carroll, Lewis 87
Carrington, Alexis 42
Cayce, Edgar 67
children 4, 14f, 17, 19, 22ff, 31ff,
  36f, 39, 40-45, 51-57, 61-68,
  79ff, 86, 90-96

colic 89
communication 35, 39, 45, 52,
  54, 100ff
concern 14, 17, 19, 22, 24, 31,
  57, 81, 102
conflict 13
confrontation 39
Cosmos 66
countertransference 71, 100, 103

D

Damian 66
death 90
delta waves 86
depression 37
desires 29, 53, 84
diagnosis 66, 68
Dickens, Charles 79, 81
DNA 75
dream catcher 14, 53f, 61ff
dream therapy 66

E

Egypt 65, 83
embarrassment 39
emotions 23, 37, 43, 66f, 101ff
essence 58, 68, 75ff, 95
event 41, 49, 98

F

fantasy 76
father 109
fatigue 37, 55
fear 14, 19, 39, 43, 47, 53, 63,
  69, 79ff, 91, 93, 95f, 100

feelings 13, 14f, 17ff, 21-27, 29ff, 35f, 39-46, 49, 53ff, 58, 63, 68f, 71, 73, 75-82, 90-93, 95-103
final words 76
food 92
Frazer, J. G. 83
Freud, Sigmund 67, 84
frustration 37, 93

G

genius 109
ghosts 62
Ginsberg, Allen 76
gravity 18
Grief 90
growth 37
guilt 26, 39, 98
Guinea 83

H

Hazlitt, William 76
headache 37, 90
health 37, 65ff
Hippocrates 66
Hoffman, E.T.A. 79
hopelessness 26
hormone 37
hostility 72
hypnic myoclonia 85

I

Iago 42
illness 14, 46, 50, 65ff
immune system 91
insomnia 37, 92
irritability 37

J

Jacob 83f
jealousy 72
Joseph 83
Jung, Carl 67, 84f

K

Koan 36

L

Lewis, C. S. 80
Lord Nelson 76
loss 27, 40, 77

M

manipulation 36, 39-47, 49, 72f, 89, 95, 101, 103
Medusa 43
memory 30, 47
mind 21f, 30, 36, 45, 52, 56, 65ff, 75, 77, 84, 96f, 101
mood 14, 18, 21, 35
movie 17ff, 23, 30, 52, 96, 100
muscle 85f
mythology 43

N

Native Americans 62, 67
night terror 36, 44, 86, 90
nightmare 23f, 31, 36, 51, 54-58, 62ff, 79, 81f, 84, 90, 92f
noise 91, 93

O

Othello 42

P

parents 14f, 17, 19, 22f, 31ff, 36, 39-47, 50-58, 63, 68, 83, 89f, 93, 95
Perseus 43
Plato 66
pons 86
problem 13f, 18, 24, 29ff, 35, 42, 45, 63f, 68f, 81f, 91f, 97ff, 103
psychoanalysis 102
psychoanalyst 67, 73, 83f, *see also* analyst
puberty 37

R

REM 54, 56, 63, 85f, 92f
Rhodes, Cecil 76

S

Sandak, Maurice 79
separation anxiety 64
sex 23, 27, 65
Shakespeare 31, 42, 77
shamans 66, 83
sleep 19, 22f, 31, 35ff, 43-47,
  51, 53-58, 62-66, 76, 83, 85f,
  89-93, 96, 101ff
  - deprivation 37, 89, 92
  - disorders 37, 64
  - disturbances 90, 92f
  - talking 57
  - terrors 64,
    see also night terror
  - walking 64, 86
sleepiness 37, 93
slips of the tongue 65, 76f, 84
society 81
Socrates 77
somniloquence 57
spirits 62, 84
struggle 13ff, 17, 21-25, 33, 35f,
  47, 51, 55, 68, 79, 92, 95, 97f,
  102f
symbol 22, 36, 85

T

talent 77
tantrum 37
teeth grinding 84, 90
television 17, 23, 42f, 92f
thalamus 86
thought 13f, 19, 21-27, 30f, 35ff,
  39, 41, 44, 49, 51f, 54, 62,
  67f, 71f, 75ff, 85, 89, 92, 95,
  97f, 100, 102f
time 18, 22, 31, 39, 49, 54f, 62f,
  66, 75, 80, 84ff, 89f, 93, 96

transference 71f, 100ff

U

unconscious 13ff, 17ff, 21-24,
  30ff, 35f, 40, 42, 44f, 51ff,
  57ff, 63, 65, 67ff, 75ff, 82,
  84f, 89, 92-98, 101ff
  - collective 67, 84

V

violence 23

W

Wilde, Oscar 76
wisdom 62, 66
wishes 17, 19, 29, 43, 51, 99

Y

Yeats, W. B. 76

Around the Subject

The Author

Dr. Ruth Velikovsky Sharon learned at the desk of her distinguished father, Dr. Immanuel Velikovsky, a prominent psychiatrist and eminent man of science whose genius engaged even the mind of his friend and contemporary, Albert Einstein.
Dr. Sharon received a B.A and M.A. degrees from New York University and a Ph.D. from the Union Institute and University. She is a graduate of the Center for Modern Psychoanalytic Studies and a certified psychoanalyst.
Among Dr. Sharon's works are two books about her father: "The Glory and the Torment", and "The Truth Behind the Torment", which chronicles the controversy surrounding her father's extraordinary scientific theories. Co-author of a book about a new understanding of parenting: "The More You Explain, the Less They Understand" and co-author of the popular book "I Refuse to Raise a Brat".

The More You Explain ...
The Less They Understand

by Ruth Velikovsky Sharon, Ph.D.

ISBN 978-1-906833-00-8

In this, perhaps the most encompassing of her works, Dr. Ruth Velikovsky Sharon brilliantly lifts the veil that shrouds the mystery of psychoanalysis, revealing intrinsic truths that can forever assist us in our journey to self-discovery and growth.

Harvard Medical School trained, Dr. John C. Seed's contribution of the Physical Health chapter will enlighten the medical community as well as the average reader, and if abided by, will help prolong life.

Imagine Art

Works of Art by Ruth Velikovsky Sharon, Ph.D. and Elisheva Velikovsky

ISBN 978-1-906833-02-2

The name of Velikovsky is mainly known from the scientific and historical discoveries of Dr. Immanuel Velikovsky.

Far less known is the artistic dimension in the Velikovsky family, mainly expressed by Elisheva (or "Elis") Velikovsky and Ruth Velikovsky Sharon, PhD., the wife and daughter of Immanuel Velikovsky. For everyone interested in and fond of visual and plastic arts this booklet will give an exhaustive overview of the remarkable range of the works of these two artists.

ABA – The Glory and the Torment

by Ruth Velikovsky Sharon, Ph.D.

ISBN 978-1-906833-20-6

In this book you get to know Immanuel Velikovsky as a person. His daughter Ruth describes his childhood, his family environment and his eventful life. Using plenty of background information, numerous anecdotes and many photographs she makes us familiar with her father, but also shows the personal dimension of the devastating campaign he encountered to in the last decades of his life.

The Truth Behind the Torment

by Ruth Velikovsky Sharon, Ph.D.

ISBN 978-1-906833-21-3

In this supplement to her father's biography, Ruth Velikovsky Sharon, PhD. depicts the true facts about the campaign against him. She publishes revealing letters in full length, that show the true nature of the undeserving - unscientific - treatment of Velikovsky by the scientific establishment, a treatment that appears rather medieval than enlightened.

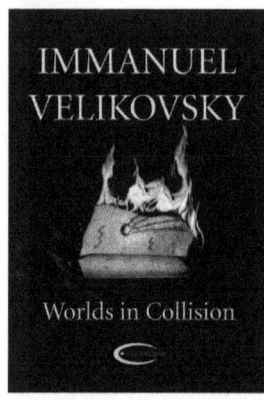

Worlds in Collision

by Immanuel Velikovsky

ISBN 978-1-906833-11-4

With this book Immanuel Velikovsky first presented the revolutionary results of his 10-year-long interdisciplinary research to the public - and caused an uproar that is still going on today.
Worlds in Collision - written in a brilliant, easily understandable and entertaining style and full to the brim with precise information - can be considered one of the most important and most challenging books in the history of science. Not without reason was this book found open on Einstein's desk after his death.

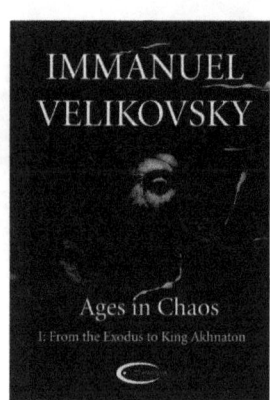

Ages in Chaos

by Immanuel Velikovsky

ISBN 978-1-906833-13-8

This is the first volume of the series *Ages in Chaos*, which undertakes a reconstruction of the history of antiquity.
With utmost precision and the exciting style of a presentation that's typical for him Immanuel Velikovsky shows what nobody would consider possible: In the conventional history of Egypt – and therefore also of many neighboring cultures – a span of 600 years is described, which has never happened! This assertion is as unbelievable and outrageous as the assertions in *Worlds in Collision* or *Earth in Upheaval*. But in the end you do not only wonder how conventional historiography has come into existence, but why it is still taught and published.

Earth in Upheaval

by Immanuel Velikovsky

ISBN 978-1-906833-12-1

After the publication of *Worlds in Collision* Immanuel Velikovsky was confronted with the argument that in the shape of the earth and in the flora and fauna there are no traces of the natural catastrophes he had described. Therefore a few years later he published *Earth in Upheaval* which not only supports the historical documents by very impressive geological and paleontological material, but even arrives at the same conclusions just based on the testimony of stones and bones.

Mankind in Amnesia

by Immanuel Velikovsky

ISBN 978-1-906833-16-9

Immanuel Velikovsky called this book the "fulfillment of his oath of Hippocrates – to serve humanity." In this book he returns to his roots as a psychologist and psychoanalytical therapist, yet not with a single person as his patient but with humanity as a whole. After an extremely revealing overview of the foundations of the various psychoanalytical systems he takes the step into crowd psychology and reopens the case of *Worlds in Collision* from a totally different point of view: a psychoanalytical case study. This way he shows that the blatant reactions to his theories (which are still going on today) have not been surprising but actually inevitable from a psychological perspective.

www.ingramcontent.com/pod-product-compliance
Lightning Source LLC
Chambersburg PA
CBHW032129090426
42743CB00007B/534